D1028744

The Underground Gourmet

by Milton Glaser & Jerome Snyder

Simon and Schuster, New York

To
GGS
and
SGG

Published by Simon and Schuster
Rockefeller Center, 630 Fifth Avenue
New York, New York 10020

FOURTH PRINTING

Library of Congress
Catalog Card Number: 67-28039
Manufactured in the
United States of America

The authors wish to thank
the *World Journal Tribune* for permission
to reprint the following articles:
"The Emergence of the Cuchifrito,"
"Dim-Sum Luncheon,"
"The Soul of Princess Pamela," and
"Yonah Schimmel vs. the Mock Knish."

ERRATA

The unparalleled rate of change that is characteristic of New York has had its inevitable effect on *The Underground Gourmet.* Since the first edition, only a month or so ago, the following events have occurred:

THE CHAMPLAIN (page 42), one of the treasured few French restaurants in our book and a New York institution, has been forced to close down with no plans to reopen. The buildings in the area from 50th Street to 47th Street west of the Avenue of the Americas (Sixth Avenue) are being razed to make way for new office structures. The demolition has also uprooted the HELLENIC PALACE (page 68), but happily it will relocate at 250 West 27th Street (989-9122), with its opening scheduled for late January. Prices and menu will remain the same as before.

IL FARO (page 76) has moved eastward to somewhat fancier quarters at 325 East 14th Street, but prices and menu remain virtually unchanged.

The INDIA PAKISTAN (page 79) *does* have a telephone. Quite mysteriously it vanished from our rating chart into the body of the review, right after the address. To repeat, the number is 864-9419.

TRINI (page 199) has changed its name to FRINI. The management is now in the hands of the former owner's nephew who is Mexican-Hawaiian and bears the unlikely name of Al Smith. The original chef is still there and the menu remains the same with one or two additions—Venezuelan arepa (a stuffed cornbread) and empanadas (meat-filled turnovers). Some of the prices are unchanged but, in general, dishes are priced about 10 to 20 percent above their previous level. The 99-cent lunch is no longer available. The new decor, more elaborate, includes familiar bullfight posters and a flamenco guitarist who performs Wednesday, Friday, Saturday and Sunday evenings.

—M. G. & J. S.
January 1968

CONTENTS

SHORT TAKES

The Underground Gourmet

No city equals New York in its fantastic assortment of good, cheap restaurants. The *Underground Gourmet* is an effort to select and evaluate some of the most interesting dining bargains the city has to offer. In the main, these restaurants were found through the process of trial and error. Our greatest rewards were found in New York's diverse ethnic pockets. Ethnic neighborhoods are knowledgeable about their national cuisine and establish the standards of their indigenous eating places. A Hungarian restaurant run by a Hungarian and frequented by the residents of a Hungarian community will invariably serve a good bowl of goulash at the right price. Other nationalities in this city exercise the same kind of control.

When we began work on this book two years ago, our intention was to find restaurants where a good meal could be had for $2.00 or less. Since that time, the cost of living has increased, and as a consequence we now find that a few of the restaurants originally listed have gone slightly beyond our desired limit. Those restaurants that still represent good value despite the increase have been retained in this book.

In the name of efficiency, urban life seems to have an unremitting tendency to eliminate that which is uniquely personal. It is extremely difficult for the owner of a small restaurant to withstand the pull of the time which favors the big, efficient, anonymous eating place; yet it is this embattled proprietor who at his best offers the qualities that are fundamental to the city's vitality and livability. The cheap, good restaurant, ethnic or not, is an indispensable part of the character of New York and, like other treasured landmarks, should be preserved.

In the pursuit of these restaurants we experienced two major satisfactions: one, the range and variety of interesting and inventively prepared foods that are available to all and that we had never before tasted; two, the pleasant confirmation of our objective—that in one of the most expensive cities in the world, a cheap and very good gastronomic life can be found for those adventurous enough to seek it out

Milton Glaser and Jerome Snyder, New York, 1967

Telephone: UN 4-5970	
Days Open: 6 days (Closed Monday)	
Hours Open: 11 A.M. to 11 P.M.	
Bar: No	
Air Conditioning: Yes	
Recommended for: Lunch. Dinner. Dating.	
Your Comments:	
Food: Good	
Ambiance: Fair to Good	
Hygiene: Good	
Service: Good	

Aki, 420 W. 119th Street, is one of the largest and oldest Japanese restaurants in New York. It is located somewhat unconventionally on the ground floor of a large apartment house in the vicinity of Columbia University. Because of its reasonable prices and comfortable surroundings, Aki is well patronized by many Columbia students and faculty members. The dining room is square, spacious and slightly overdecorated with Japanese ornamentation. The menu features a dazzling array of 16 dinner combinations, most of which are priced around $1.75 and in one case goes only as high as $3.50. Each complete dinner consists of a choice of clear or soybean soup, sunomono (salad) rice and a choice of dessert. The main dish determines the price and establishes the beautiful-sounding title by which it may be ordered. Yamakahe is grated yam with a filet of tunafish ($1.75). Yosenabe is a casserole of mixed vegetables with a choice of chicken, fish or shrimp. Sushi, a pretty dish consisting of raw fish, seaweed and cold rice, is $1.75 (author's choice). Udon includes a choice of raw egg, chicken and egg, fish cake and vegetables or tempura over a bowl of noodles ($1.75). Teriyaki, is a dish of sliced beef, pork, chicken or fish marinated in soy sauce, then broiled ($1.75). Donburi is composed of either beef, pork, chicken or shrimp with beaten egg served over a large bowl of rice ($1.75). Eel (unagi) is $.25 more. Slightly higher in price are the Butadofu, pork with bean curd, and the Tonkatsu, a pork cutlet, both at $2.25. Dessert for all combinations is a choice of fruit cup, fortune cookies or ice cream, and, needless to say, tea in copious quantity comes with everything. There is an à la carte menu with essentially the same dishes as the dinner, but these seem to represent lesser value. Two Ochazuke dishes (hot tea over a rice, vegetable and meat bowl) are worth a mention, both at $1.50. Waitresses are attractive and in sufficient number.

If you are a Japanese food lover or find yourself in that uptown area, Aki presents an especially convenient and good restaurant.

Telephone:	243-9322
Days Open:	7 days
Hours Open:	11:30 A.M. to 10:30 P.M.
Bar:	No
Air Conditioning:	Yes
Recommended for:	Lunch. Dinner. Dating.
Your Comments:	
Food:	Good
Ambiance:	Good
Hygiene:	Fair
Service:	Good

Asia de Cuba, 190 Eighth Avenue, (21st Street), is one in a chain of three Chinese-Spanish restaurants, the other two being the Asia Pearl and the Asia Star.

The Sino-Latin restaurant is a comparatively recent phenomenon on the New York eating scene. Cuba had one of the largest Chinese populations in the Western Hemisphere. Since the revolution, many operators of Chinese restaurants in Cuba have come here with their cooks and personnel. This unexpected culinary hybrid is one of the benefits of the immigration.

The Asia de Cuba is a small, clean, functional, luncheonette-type restaurant. It has a counter which seats 10 and table space for 35. In Sino-Latin cooking the two styles are not joined. What really happens is that one can choose from two menus, with very pleasant results. The Chinese soup is a standout at 45 cents. This dish is a rich broth with meat, bean sprouts, noodles; shortly before serving, a raw egg is added to poach in the liquid. The Chinese side of the menu is neither extensive nor particularly unusual. Some of the items include a beef lo mein ($1.35), lobster egg foo young ($1.85), fried wontons (45 cents), small beans with meat (85 cents). Peculiarly enough, Asia de Cuba's Spanish-speaking Chinese cook seems more at home with the Cuban dishes. Picadillo, an authors' choice (70 cents), is a flavorful combination of spiced chopped meat with olives, peppers and onions, served with saffron rice in a generous portion. Rice and shrimp, a Caribbean standby, is well prepared. There are some unusual omelets available, among which are a plantain (60 cents), Spanish sausage (70 cents), and potato (60 cents). Other typical Cuban dishes include fried chick-peas (40 cents), yellow rice and chicken ($1.25) and fried plantains (35 cents).

The desserts are almost exclusively Spanish. Small Latin restaurants rarely miss with their flan (egg custard with caramel sauce), and Asia de Cuba's is excellent at 25 cents. An unusual item is a very sweet pudding called Dorma in Ciel (sleeping in heaven) for 25 cents which is well worth trying. The espresso, aromatically fresh, is very good and a buy at 15 cents.

Although clientele of Asia de Cuba is mainly Spanish-speaking, the management is especially gracious and tries to make all visitors feel quite comfortable.

Telephone:	LE 5-3700
Days Open:	Monday through Friday
Hours Open:	Noon to 3 P.M. (Lunch only)
Bar:	No
Air Conditioning:	No
Recommended for:	Lunch. Dating.
Your Comments:	
Food:	Good
Ambiance:	Good
Hygiene:	Good
Service:	Excellent

The Atran Cultural Center Restaurant, 25 E. 78th Street, is deep in an unlikely building in an unlikely part of the city. On the northwest corner of 78th Street and Madison Avenue in an area of fashionable art galleries, fashionable shops and fashionable restaurants is hidden a truly out-of-the-ordinary dining room. One enters a former East Side mansion (78th Street side) marked simply "Atran Center for Jewish Culture." You walk across a small marbleized lobby, open an unmarked door, follow a bilingual directional finger that says "Dining Room," down the stairs, turn right into a narrow, long hallway and enter the year 1935.

The dining room, square and plain, seats about 50 people at oilcloth-covered tables. Seated at these tables are a cross-section of Jewish intelligentsia (male and female) of another era, young social workers, artists, students and an occasional art dealer. The atmosphere is homey and the air is filled with lively conversation. At the far end of the room is a short counter that looks in on a small kitchen. The food is prepared and served in cafeteria style by two gracious ladies, Helen Henig and Frances Sperber, who have been with the restaurant for 13 years. Time has not dimmed their pleasant and attentive manner.

The bill of fare is posted on a blackboard adjoining the serving counter, and it consists of dishes of authentic middle-European Jewish home cooking. The menu varies from day to day, and there is always a home-style soup (25 cents) on hand, such as thick mushroom, barley, vegetable, split pea or potato. Soup is one of the assets of Jewish cooking, and the Atran holds fast to that cherished tradition. Other dishes available are gefülte fish (95 cents), roast chicken ($1.00), potted meat (95 cents), stuffed cabbage (90 cents), boiled fish (85 cents). The carbohydrate-laden accompaniments might be kasha (browned buckwheat groats), oven-browned potatoes and noodle or potato pudding. These are all very good. One of the flaws in Jewish cuisine, however, is the lack of feeling in the preparation of fresh green vegetables. Here too the Atran cleaves to tradition.

Other good dishes are an excellent chopped liver (25 cents) and fresh egg salad (20 cents). The desserts are simple, rather plaintive but tasty home-made cookies, apple sauce, baked apple.

Coffee is good, though the In drink is a glass of scalding hot water, a wedge of lemon and a tea bag.

The Atran is open only from 8 A.M. to 4 P.M., Monday through Friday. There is a comfort and a warming nostalgia that make this unpretentious dining room a rare find.

Telephone:	SP 7-1930
Days Open:	6 days (Closed Sunday)
Hours Open:	4:30 A.M. to midnight
Bar:	No
Air Conditioning:	Yes
Recommended for:	Breakfast. Lunch. Dinner. Dating?
Your Comments:	
Food:	Good to Excellent
Ambiance:	Good
Hygiene:	Fair to Good
Service:	Good

The B & H, 127 Second Avenue (at St. Mark's Place), may be New York's best dairy luncheonette. The dairy restaurant has its origins in the orthodox Jewish dietary tradition of separating meat as an ingredient from all milk products. This culinary delineation goes as far as separating the dishes and utensils used in the cooking as well as the food. The dairy restaurant remains a part of the kosher heritage. It is implied assurance that its cuisine is free from any violation of the Jewish culinary code. The limitation of ingredients gives rise to a range of menu inventions such as vegetarian chopped liver (one of the best-held recipe secrets in dairy-luncheonette cabal) and protose steak, a hamburger made of vegetables. Then too there are variations on a vegetable theme—vegetable roast, mushroom cutlet, etc. These dishes require a somewhat openminded approach on the part of the diner, but some—and the vegetarian chopped liver (authors' choice) in particular—can become a delicious addiction. The vegetarian adaptations, however, constitute only a small part of the B & H repertoire. For a start there are always two muscular soups on the menu culled from a list that includes mushroom and barley, cabbage, potato, Yankee bean and the superb matzoh ball soup (available only on Friday and an authors' choice). The matzoh ball, as the name indicates, is a dumpling made of softened, virtually pulverized matzoh; in this case it reposes in a magnificent pseudo-chicken consommé. Finally, there are three beautiful summer treats: a fruit soup, cold borscht, (a thin beet soup), and schav, a bitter, sour-grass soup. In the egg group, many unusual dishes may be found. There are omelets such as lox (smoked salmon) and finely chopped onions, farmer cheese (a pressed cottage cheese), fresh mushroom and matzoh brie, a hybrid pancake made of egg and matzoh. Matzoh brie, a versatile dish, may be eaten with salt, sugar, jam or syrup, as taste dictates. Fish is given its proper place on the B & H menu. You can choose among boiled carp, pike, baked whitefish in tomato and green pepper sauce and on Friday and Saturday a first-rate hot or cold gefülte fish is served with the traditional accompaniment of strong horse-radish and a firm boiled potato. Further along you can indulge in pirogen (see page 95) served either boiled or fried, and a set of formidable cheese blintzes. For the appropriate dishes, side dishes include kashe, egg barley and a variety of overcooked vegetables, the traditional weakness of Jewish cooking. Salads, however, are always fresh and of high quality. The sandwich category, normally taken for granted, has attained new levels of distinction at the B & H. Take rich, fresh, dark pumpernickel, corn bread, bagels, bialystok rolls, or onion rolls with sweet butter applied to both sides, enclosing layers of fresh ingredients, and you have an achievement of kitchen art.

Physically, the B & H packs a lot of food and people in a very small area. A narrow store with a counter that seats about 12 and a short string of tables that are almost impossible to eat at in comfort gives it an appearance that is at best undistinguished. The B & H is always busy from 4 A.M. to 11 P.M. and closed on Sunday. The clientele is as mixed as the bubbling neighborhood: artists, writers, actors, cabbies, workingmen, and indigenous Jewish patriarchs and matriarchs.

Behind the counter the scene is a good-natured, crowded, steaming, pushing, sloppy storm of activity. Despite the welter of arms, legs and shouted orders, the service is fast and efficient. The B & H is no place to go for a leisurely meal, but the brusque good spirits of the proprietors, the fascinating admixture of customers and the peerless quality of its food make it a place in which eating is a genuine happening.

Telephone:	684-8195
Days Open:	7 days
Hours Open:	Noon to 9:30 P.M.
Bar:	No
Air Conditioning:	Yes
Recommended for:	Lunch. Dinner. Dating.
Your Comments:	
Food:	Good
Ambiance:	Fair to Good
Hygiene:	Fair to Good
Service:	Good

The Bagdad Restaurant, 4 W. 28th Street, is one of five Middle Eastern restaurants in its immediate area. This concentration of restaurants, with the addition of three on Atlantic Avenue in Brooklyn, represent the sum of Arabic cooking in the city. An unusually high percentage of them have found their place in the *Underground Gourmet* because they serve good food at good value.

In general, Syrian cooking has a distant relationship to the Armenian and Greek styles. Lamb is ever-present in multiple forms. Rice is the principal carbohydrate and the familiar accompanying vegetables are eggplant, okra, squash, string beans and spinach. The basic cooking technique is stewing, and olive oil is used freely. But there are enough dishes unique to the Syrian cuisine to make it distinctive.

The Bagdad, up one flight of stairs, is a large, homey, pleasant room with big windows overlooking a street that houses a number of small stores dealing in notions and novelties. The tablecloths are crisp and white and the walls are punctuated with an unlikely mélange of paintings ranging from abstract expressionism to academic naturalism. The owner-cook, Mr. George Zarbatany, is solicitious about his patrons' preference and will visit your table in order to discuss the day's bill of fare and then return to his kitchen duties. Two classic Syrian appetizers, hommus (60 cents) and baba ganou (70 cents), described on page 40, are both very good here. Brain salad (80 cents), another standby, is excellent but extraordinarily high in cholesterol. Tabouli (75 cents), a cold salad of parsley, tomatoes and cooked bulgar wheat, is especially tasty. There is a full compliment of stewed lamb dishes with varying vegetables. These include artichokes with meat, fava beans with meat, mushrooms with meat, string beans with meat, all at $1.10. You can find a raft of boiled lamb-organ meats too, including heart ($1.00), kidney ($1.00), liver ($1.20), sweetbreads ($1.50) and fries (testes) for $1.50. Kibby, a chopped lamb and bulgar wheat mixture with pine nuts, is served both raw ($1.00) and baked ($1.10). On Thursday a stuffed oval-shaped kibby in laban (a thin yogurt sauce) is offered at $1.50 (an authors' choice). Wednesday's feature is stuffed tripe. This triangular-shaped tripe pocket is filled with a steamy mixture of rice, chick-peas and ground meat ($1.50), also an authors' choice. Filling out the entrée list are spinach pies ($1.00) and shish kebab ($2.00). Syrians have a fine feeling for the virtues of fresh cold vegetables, and the Bagdad lists a nice range, such as celery (40 cents), hearts of lettuce (40 cents), sliced cucumber (40 cents), sliced tomatoes (40 cents), pickles, radishes and scallions (20 cents), black olives (35 cents).

A Syrian table is always graced with an abundance of lemon wedges and Holy Land (unleavened) bread, both fresh and toasted. The Bagdad offers a rather disappointing selection of pastries, but, seasonally fresh fruit is served, a pleasant ending to a Middle Eastern meal. Either American coffee or the thicker Syrian demitasse is available and good.

Telephone: 986-6678	
Days Open: 6 days (Closed Sunday)	
Hours Open: 9 A.M. to midnight	
Bar: Beer only	
Air Conditioning: Yes	
Recommended for: Lunch. Dinner. Dating.	
Your Comments:	
Food: Good to Excellent	
Ambiance: Fair to Good	
Hygiene: Good to Excellent	
Service: Good	

Belcrep (a portmanteau word made of the words "Belgium" and "crêpe"), 47 W. 44th Street, is centrally located on a street distinguished by the Harvard Club but otherwise quite ordinary. The Belcrep is a recent addition to a small group of restaurants devoted to the preparation of the crêpe (a wafer-thin pancake) in all its variations. This type of restaurant, so well known in Paris and Brussels, has made its appearance in New York only within the last few years.

Belcrep is unexpectedly large and is something of a cross between a luncheonette and a restaurant. The long curving counter occupies the forward section and tables fill the rear.

Crêpe, the only entrée on the menu, made either of buckwheat or wheat (white) flour, is offered in a staggering 105 choices. The prices range from 40 cents for the plain unadorned crêpe to $2.50 for one of the more exotic numbers, such as crêpe with imported goose liver, caviar or Belgian-style whipped cream. Fortunately the major part of the menu is far more modest, and moderate in price. The crêpes are thin and supple and the fillings fresh and of high quality. The authors will not pretend that they have eaten their way through all of the 105 permutations, but some that strike one's fancy include crêpe with snail butter (65 cents), with eggs and cheese ($1.15), eggs, bacon and spinach ($1.50), seafood curry ($1.95), creamed chicken ($1.60), onions (95 cents), tomatoes country style ($1.25), ice cream and apples ($1.25), roquefort (95 cents) and with apples ($1.25), almond cream ($1.60). The *grandemère* of all crêpes: suzette with Grand Marnier, Kirsch, Cognac, all flambé ($1.95).

Under the dessert heading is a list of light Belgian waffles with an assortment of toppings. A sample cholesterol fantasy consists of the waffle, sugar, home-made whipped cream and burnt-almond flavor (75 cents). The home-made ice cream is superb, and a scoop goes for 25 cents; a sundae is 65 cents and a mysterious item called white dame is $1.25.

Belcrep is not a Frenchman's restaurant. The crêpes, though of excellent quality, are not overly substantial. Of course one can fill up with desserts, but this is neither nutritionally nor economically sound, for the bill can go up fairly quickly.

The house coffee, called café au go-go for reasons known only to the proprietor, is great and refilled for free; it costs only 15 cents. Espresso is available at 25 cents and Belgian filter coffee at 30 cents. Waitresses are either French or Belgian, and they maintain a competent standard of Continental service.

Telephone:	864-9634
Days Open:	6 days (Closed Tuesday)
Hours Open:	Th., F., Sat., noon to 2 A.M.; M., W., Sun., noon to midnight
Bar:	No
Air Conditioning:	Yes
Recommended for:	Lunch. Dinner. Dating?
Your Comments:	
Food:	Fair to Good
Ambiance:	Fair
Hygiene:	Good
Service:	Fair to Good

The Bombay India, 465 W. 125th Street, is a modest Harlem restaurant with a good selection of curries. Mr. Eshadali, the proprietor and cook, is from Pakistan and has presided over his unpretentious enterprise for the past nine years. The Bombay India, near a city-housing complex, is installed in a narrow store with a recently refurbished dining room which has a simple and neat appearance. The emphasis, however, is on food, and the Bombay India à la carte menu offers an assortment of 28 curries—56 if you consider that each curry may be had with either rooty (a soft, fried Indian bread) or alu paratha (a somewhat larger, griddle-fried flat bread made with potatoes) and a choice of yellow or white rice. Any curry order comes with a separate portion of Indian bread, a dish of dall (a curry-seasoned cabbage dish) and a hot sauce. Lamb curry consisting of cleanly trimmed chunks of lamb in a tasty curry sauce, with rooty ($1.35) or with paratha, brings the price up to $1.70 (authors' choice). A sampling of the rest of the menu includes egg curry rooty ($1.45), paratha ($1.80); chicken curry rooty ($1.35), paratha ($1.65); beef curry for $1.65 (trimmed chunks of beef), with paratha ($2.00); fish curry ($1.30), with paratha ($1.65); vegetable curry with white rice ($1.20)—10 cents more for yellow rice. The bona dishes are the hotter variety and come with rice as well as bread. The surcharge of 10 cents for yellow (saffron) rice applies to all curries. A side order of rooty costs 50 cents, while paratha is 70 cents. Two other uncommon curry dishes are the combined liver and heart curry with rooty ($1.30), or paratha ($1.65); and the kima curry (a ground-meat version) at $1.30 or $1.70, depending on whether it comes with rooty or paratha. Appetizers or somoza are limited to beef, lamb or vegetable, which is enclosed in a crisp, deep-fat-fried dough. Mango chutney or green mango pickle (extremely hot) are 30 cents. Mr. Eshadali prepares his curries on the milder side and with a light hand, but a side dish of hot sauce is served. The components come to the table in separate small dishes and make an attractive offering. Desserts are somewhat commonplace. Ice cream is 20 cents, rasso goola (a sweet cheese ball in sauce) is 20 cents, and halwoa is 25 cents—a dark farina pudding which should not be confused with the common halvah. Coffee is 15 cents, Indian tea is 20 cents, and ginger beer is 25 cents. The staff is limited to one waitress, but the service is adequate.

The Bombay India is an unpretentious restaurant with a simple specialty: the curry dish, which it prepares and serves well and at a reasonable price.

Telephone:	PL 7-9352
Days Open:	6 days (Closed Sunday)
Hours Open:	Noon to 10 P.M.
Bar:	Wine and beer
Air Conditioning:	Yes
Recommended for:	Lunch. Dinner. Dating.
Your Comments:	
Food:	Good to Excellent
Ambiance:	Fair to Good
Hygiene:	Fair to Good
Service:	Good

The Columbia Hotel, 70 W. 46th Street, which houses the Brazilian Coffee Restaurant, also has as residents many Brazilian and Portuguese tourists. That they regularly dine at the Brazilian Coffee Restaurant is a tribute to its authenticity and value. It is the opinion of the authors that this small restaurant represents one of the best values in New York. Portuguese-Brazilian cooking is exotic (there are only three other restaurants of this genre in New York), but even the most timid gastronome will find many dishes to suit his taste.

The Brazilian Coffee Restaurant is an unpretentious room with an aerial photo mural of Rio de Janeiro at the rear and some pseudo-modern late-Matisse-like murals on the side wall. It seats about 50 people, and the tables are always neatly appointed, with white tablecloths and white cloth napkins. Decor aside, the issue here is food. Upon first being served, one is struck by the quality of the ingredients, the excellence of the cooking and the generosity of the portions. A civilized touch is the practice of bringing the food to the table on serving dishes.

There are a few first-course dishes, such as Portuguese sardines and soup and melon (50 cents each), but in view of the large entrée portions you would be well advised to pass them up. Some twenty separate entrées comprise the à la carte menu, more than half of which are in the *Underground Gourmet* price range. In addition there is a special of the day, which is always excellent and well worth trying. Some of the outstanding specialties are a beef jardinera, a Portuguese potted beef with properly cooked vegetables (served on Monday, $1.95); a magnificently prepared loin of pork (Tuesday, $2.00); Wednesday and Saturday feature feijoada, the Brazilian national dish (an authors' choice). This is one of the few dishes here that may offer some gustatory obstacles, but it is supremely rewarding. Feijoada is a black-bean casserole dish prepared with generous pieces of pork, sausage and pig's ears. It comes served in a steaming brown crock and is accompanied by separate dishes of rice and greens, orange wedges and farofa, a toasted farina. Although feijoada costs $2.50, the quantity is ample for two. One of the great fried chicken dishes of the world is BCR's chicken bossa nova (a crisp fried chicken loaded with garlic flavor and cholesterol). The churrasco, a fine bit of beef tastefully broiled, is as good as you can get in this city, and only $1.95 (an authors' choice). Other good dishes: veal cutlet a Portuguesa ($1.80), picadinho (ground spiced meat with egg) for $1.75, baked cod fish ($1.90).

Nothing on this menu falls below a consistently high standard. All entrées are handsomely served with an accompaniment of large dishes of rice, black beans and salad. A nice addition for the affluent is a bottle of cold vinho verde, a Portuguese light green wine, half-bottle for $1.55. There is a wide choice of other excellent Portuguese wines at reasonable prices. Desserts are not notable, but the coffee is good. Service tends to slow up a bit when the restaurant is crowded, but the red-jacketed waiters are unfailingly attentive and courteous. All in all, the BCR is a very good small restaurant.

Telephone:	582-8510
Days Open:	7 days
Hours Open:	10:30 A.M. to 11 P.M.
Bar:	No
Air Conditioning:	Yes
Recommended for:	Lunch. Dinner. Dating.
Your Comments:	
Food:	Good to Excellent
Ambiance:	Good to Excellent
Hygiene:	Good
Service:	Excellent

The Cabana Carioca, 123 W. 45th Street, is the most recently established of the three Brazilian restaurants in the West Forties. These restaurants share in common a wide range of unusual and attractive dishes at reasonable prices. In addition, a specially Brazilian friendly spirit permeates all three. The Brazilian style of cooking has many of the features of Spanish, Portuguese and various South American cuisines. The Brazilian quality comes from its extensive range of ingredients and the imaginative way in which all the elements are combined. This approach is best exemplified in feijoada. At The Cabana Carioca this dish contains dried beef, sausages, fresh pork cooked with black beans served with fried cales (kale), orange slices and farina ($2.50 and an authors' choice). The owner confidently claims that two Americans cannot finish one order. Their tripe is stewed with sausages, potatoes served with rice, beans and farofa—farina—($2.00), and the black-bean pudding is made with creamed mandioca (a tropical plant used as a thickening) served with cales, sausages and rice ($2.00). The large menu is divided into "Day by Day" specialties, quick orders, chicken, fish, seafood and egg dishes. On Tuesdays, picadinho—seasoned ground beef, fried egg, rice and beans—is served for $1.50, or oxtail with a creamed sauce, rice and beans for $1.75. The accompanying beans are of the small, rich, dark-brown variety; they easily become an addiction. On Wednesday chicken liver and gizzards stewed with sweet peas served with rice and beans ($1.50) or beef stew with potatoes and the expected accompaniment is served for $1.75 (authors' choice). In the main, the quick orders are steaks and chops. The prices range from $2.00 for a grilled veal chop to $3.00 for the T-bone steak, sautéed onions, rice and beans or French fries. There are five interesting chicken specialties, including chicken fried with breaded egg served with salad ($2.00) and chicken São Paulo style served with spaghetti and tomato sauce ($1.50). The Cabana Carioca has an excellent feeling for the preparation of fish dishes. Some excellent selections are fried fish with boiled potatoes ($1.50) and fried fish with sautéed onions and sweet peppers ($2.00). Under the daily specialties there is the vatapa bains, an authentic regional dish which is a sort of Brazilian bouillabaisse made of shrimp and various fish in a thick sauce ($2.25 and an authors' choice). A very good omelet, made with onions and tomatoes, is served with rice for $2.25 (authors' choice). A good and decent-sized tomato and lettuce salad (onion if desired) comes with all entrées. Small rolls are also served, and the butter comes packed in small individual jars. In those cases where the price of the dish exceeds our price limit, the authors feel that the excellent preparation and substantial size of the portion recommend the dish as an exceptional value.

An interesting side dish is the potato vegetable salad with mayonnaise ($.50). The list of meat canapés ($.25 each) also merits attention.

Desserts are tropical and extremely sweet: home-made milk caramel, papaya chunks, cocoanut custard, peaches in sauce, guava shells, guava jelly and orange pudding (all $.50). A combination platter called doce de leite, composed of many of the aforementioned plus a piece of white South American cheese is $.75. This dish should be sufficient for two or three. Good Brazilian coffee, charmingly served in a small pot ($.15), ends the meal.

As indicated earlier, the portions are unusually large and so arrayed to make them visually gratifying. The restaurant is somewhat easy to overlook, because it is one flight above street level and identified by only a small sign hanging above the doorway. Once upstairs, you will find that the room, though modestly decorated, is quite pleasant and friendly. These qualities are matched by the service.

The counter at the rear of the room is excellent for singles at lunch or dinner, and the tables near the window accommodate small groups comfortably.

Telephone:	OR 9-6755
Days Open:	7 days
Hours Open:	11 A.M. to 11 P.M.
Bar:	Yes
Air Conditioning:	Yes
Recommended for:	Lunch. Dinner. Dating.
Your Comments:	
Food:	Good
Ambiance:	Good
Hygiene:	Good
Service:	Excellent

Cedars of Lebanon, 39 E. 30th Street, is, as its name implies, a Lebanese restaurant. It is in an area that is punctuated by several other restaurants specializing in Middle Eastern food. The Cedars of Lebanon, however, is considerably better than most of its competitors. It is run efficiently by John Arege, a former Lebanese consular official who has been the sole proprietor since 1958. Mr. Arege, a solidly built man of considerable energy and articulateness, vigorously supervises all aspects of the restaurant operation. His day begins at 6:30 A.M.; he shops at the local market and travels to Atlantic Avenue in Brooklyn to obtain the special Oriental ingredients found in the Arabic enclave in that area. The result of his careful ministrations is a well-run, good-quality, inexpensive restaurant. The dining room is large, adequately lighted, clean and further brightened by the spotlessly white tablecloths. The decor consists of a cycle of poorly painted vistas of the Middle East. Every meal starts with a well-filled basket of Syrian unleavened bread and a dish of either pickled turnips, cucumbers or scallions. The bulk of entrées on the menu are generally less than $1.50. Shish kebab is the most expensive item. It comes in three styles: with onions, $2.00; with tomatoes and onions, $2.20; and plain, only $1.90. The rest of the very large menu offers an excellent Lebanese cous-cous (a restaurant variety different from the Algerian version) at $1.50. Cous-cous in the Lebanese manner is a stew of chick-peas, chicken and barley. A varicty of kibee dishes (ground lamb, wheat germ and pine nuts) is available; raw is 90 cents, baked is 90 cents. With grape leaves, mushrooms or eggplant the cost goes up to $1.30. Another rare and authentic dish is the meloukhia with chicken. The dish consists of pieces of chicken on a bed of a spinachlike vegetable (meloukhia) and broth-soaked toasted Syrian bread for $1.50 (an authors' choice). There is a good variety of appetizers, and the hommus bi takini (peanut butter ground chick-peas) and sesame oil (50 cents) and baba ghanouge (eggplant with sesame oil) for 50 cents are noteworthy. Stuffed grape leaves and cooked lamb and vegetable dishes round out the menu. A genuine bargain can be found in the special lunch, which includes a choice of four entrées, dessert and coffee for $1.50. In the realm of desserts the emphasis is on the honey-soaked pastries

(50 cents each). Mr. Arege will prepare a plate of assorted delicacies for you at the same price you would pay for one kind. Both the American and the thick Turkish coffee at 15 cents are excellent. The service is generally pleasant and prompt. The ubiquitous Mr. Arege is there at the register to take your money, compliments and comments and will, like a true diplomat, handle your complaints, if any.

SEE ERRATA, page 5

Telephone:	247-9274
Days Open:	6 days (Closed Sunday)
Hours Open:	M. through F., 11:30 A.M. to 3 P.M., 5 P.M. to 10 P.M.; Sat. 5 P.M. to midnight
Bar:	Yes
Air Conditioning:	Yes
Recommended for:	Lunch. Dinner. Dating.
Your Comments:	
Food:	Good
Ambiance:	Good
Hygiene:	Fair to Good
Service:	Fair to Good

The Champlain, 115 W. 49th Street, is in that section of the midtown theater area which has a strong honky-tonk flavor. Far from being a tourist trap, however, the Champlain is a well-established, straightforward, inexpensive, good and fairly authentic French restaurant. While there are many French restaurants in New York, very few good ones fall within the *Underground Gourmet* price limitation. The Champlain luncheon at $1.60 or $1.80 probably constitutes the best buy among the city's French restaurants. Because its location is convenient and the value good, the restaurant is always swarming with customers even though there are 211 seats available. The space is divided into two rooms, each with a somewhat different character. The front room is more informal and bistrolike, with a bar, low ceiling, wood-paneled walls and large square recessed lights, all of which creates a mood of the Thirties. The back room is spacious, high-ceilinged, has hanging chandeliers, poster-decorated brick walls and an altogether more elegant atmosphere. The food is not *haute cuisine*, but it *does* have the solid, assured quality of a Parisian neighborhood restaurant. For $1.80 (the $1.60 club luncheon omits the first course) the restaurant features an astonishing choice of 16 hors d'ouevres, 30 entrées and 22 desserts. While one would expect a low-cost luncheon of this dimension to be composed of many routine and familiar dishes, the Champlain does offer a surprising number of imaginative alternatives. Some of these choices are moules bordelaise (mussels in a wine and onion sauce), French saucisses de Toulouse with mushroom sauce (a pan-browned, spicy, pinkish, finely ground pork sausage)—an authors' choice. Other good selections include striped bass with wine sauce, filet of sole meunière, roast loin of pork, French pot roast with mushroom sauce, omelette fines herbes, beef bordelaise. For a modest premium you may have sweetbreads with sauce financière (10 cents extra), bouillabaisse Marseilles (35 cents extra), prime London broil (10 cents extra), civet de venaison (venison) for 50 cents more, fresh brook trout with sauce amandine (20 cents extra). The crêpe maison (a thin pancake stuffed with king crab Thermidor) is 75 cents extra. All the entrées come with a fresh vegetable and a potato or rice. The bread basket is well filled with a good, crusty French bread.

The appetizers are also quite interesting. There is a small plate of assorted hors d'oeuvres which includes herring, rice, white beans, pâté, cole slaw and salami. A bit tiny but tasty, pâté en gêlée and pâté Champlain are both home-made and fine-tasting dishes. Moules rémoulade, steamed mussels in a thick white sauce, egg rémoulade, baked stuffed clams run a surcharge of 10 cents. The three soups include an oignon aux croutons, a soup du jour and consommé madrilène.

The Champlain retains its variety and strength in the dessert area. Fruit rafraîchis, for example, is a good-sized dish of fresh fruit. Peach melba is a full-sized scoop of ice cream with a half a peach (canned) and a fruit sauce. One can also choose from rum, cheese or pound cake, peaches in wine, strawberry tart, Napoleon, cream pies, sherbets and ice cream and a range of cheeses, including Swiss, Camembert, Port Salut, cream, chèvre (goat) or blue. Demitasse, tea or American coffee ends the meal.

The portions in every case are ample, and the presentation is generally attractive. A glass of wine to supplement the meal is only 40 cents for a red or white domestic brand.

The Champlain is run well and the service is prompt and informal. Occasionally the service tends to get a bit slow when the room is fully crowded.

Telephone:	CH 3-9542
Days Open:	6 days (Closed Sunday)
Hours Open:	7 A.M. to 9 P.M.
Bar:	No
Air Conditioning:	Yes
Recommended for:	Breakfast. Lunch. Dinner. Dating.
Your Comments:	
Food:	Good to Excellent
Ambiance:	Good
Hygiene:	Excellent
Service:	Good

Chez Brigitte, 77 Greenwich Avenue, seats 11 at its back-to-back counter and probably qualifies as New York's smallest restaurant. Its size makes it somewhat easy to overlook in bustling Greenwich Village. That this luncheonette-type restaurant is an extremely pleasant and rewarding place is due exclusively to Louise, its diminutive proprietor and cook. A charming, lively woman from Marseilles, she brings to her cooking the special zest characteristic of that southern French port. Superb control of matters culinary is also evident in the order and cleanliness that prevail in the compact kitchen. The menu is not extensive, but all dishes the authors tried were simply and well prepared. We especially recommend the boeuf bourguignon ($1.25) and the ragout de veau ($1.25). The omelets (mushroom or cheese), a Louise specialty, are an exceptional treat at $1.00. This basic dish, prepared within a foot of where you are seated, is lightened with a dash of ice water and is cooked in pure olive oil instead of butter—a touch which bespeaks its Midi origin. Splendid! Portions are not overly large but quite sufficient. Since all the cooking is done before you, you can see that the quality of the ingredients is high and the food fresh and well chosen. Desserts are not distinguished, but there is a good home-made flan. There is a complete lack of pretension in Louise's dishes—only the rare good taste of a sensitive hand. Because the restaurant is so intimate, service cannot be bad, and Louise and two Spanish sisters (Luisa and Melina) add grace and charm. All in all, eating in this unusual, compact restaurant is a very pleasant experience.

Telephone:	929-5172
Days Open:	7 days
Hours Open:	11 A.M. to 10:30 P.M.
Bar:	No
Air Conditioning:	Yes
Recommended for:	Lunch. Dinner. Dating?
Your Comments:	
Food:	Fair to Good
Ambiance:	Fair to Good
Hygiene:	Fair to Good
Service:	Fair to Good

Dragon de Oro, 146 Eighth Avenue (between 17th and 18th streets), is another pleasant Sino-Cuban restaurant. Architecturally, the dining room is most peculiar. As one enters there is a long counter on the left, very much like any conventional luncheonette. In the right wall is a framed observation window which enables the counter patrons to look into the adjoining dining room. The entrance to the dining room is at the far end of the restaurant. Once you are in the dining room, where the observation procedure is reversed, the feeling is not unlike being in a control room looking out on a behavioral experiment in eating patterns.

As for the division of national influences in the cooking, the Chinese side is distinctly the weaker. The Chinese-style soups in general are excellent, and a big bowl of sopa China (bean sprouts, chicken livers, pork bits, bok choy and whole egg yolk, which is cooked by the heat of soup) is 50 cents (an authors' choice). There are four fried-rice dishes: arroz frito especial ($1.00), arroz frito con camarones (shrimps) for $1.25, arroz frito con pollo (chicken) for $1.25 and arroz frito Dragon de Oro ($1.30). This dish is a composite of shrimps, chicken and pork. The seven chop suey and five chow mein dishes are ordinary and tend to be overcooked. The cook, though Chinese, appears to be more at home with Cuban dishes: picadillo a la criolla (home style), a chopped-meat and greenpepper mixture (an authors' choice) at $1.00; ropa vieja (strings of stewed beef), another tasty dollar's worth, as are carne guisada (beef stew) and lengua estofada (stuffed tongue). Other good values are bistec palomella (beefsteak) y ensalada (salad) for $1.35; and liver steak (Italian style), small pieces of liver sautéed with onion ($1.10). One-quarter fried chicken is 95 cents and a half is $1.65. Both come with rice, beans and salad.

An interesting variation of the better-known Italian hero is the Cuban sandwich, which is composed of ham, pork, cheese and relish on a long, fresh roll. The entire sandwich is placed in a hot press and the sandwich is served thoroughly warmed, which improves its flavor. The desserts, fundamentally Latin American, are guava shells or marmalade with cream cheese (40 cents) and coconut strips with cheese (40 cents). Three excellent puddings are the flan, natilla and pudim diplomatico (rich pudding) at 25 cents each. The espresso is superb and only 10 cents.

There are five blue-plate specials which offer meat, poultry or fish with fried rice, lettuce and tomato. They range in price from $1.25 to $1.60.

The Dragon de Oro has a lively, busy quality characteristic of a neighborhood center. Almost at any time of the day one will find it well attended by the locals, who are virtually all Spanish-speaking. A rudimentary knowledge of Spanish is helpful, since no menu in English is available. The waiters speak enough English to lend a hand, however. Their service is quick and impersonal.

Telephone:	233-3336
Days Open:	7 days
Hours Open:	M. through F. 11 A.M. to 10 P.M.; Sat., Sun., 11 A.M. to 11 P.M.
Bar:	No
Air Conditioning:	Yes
Recommended for:	Lunch. Dinner. Dating.
Your Comments:	
Food:	Excellent
Ambiance:	Good
Hygiene:	Good
Service:	Good

On the "wrong side" of the Bowery in Chinatown at 3 East Broadway (opposite Chatham Square), the Dumpling House is one of the very few restaurants that features Mandarin style cooking. The undistinguished appearance of Dumpling House gives no indication of the variety and quality of the dishes it offers. For those accustomed to the prevalent Cantonese style of Chinese cooking the menu of this small restaurant will come as a dazzling revelation.

The menu which lists a total of 122 dishes begins impressively with a choice of 12 soups. The authors chose spinach and bean-cake, 80 cents for the medium portion which serves two very nicely; a large portion for $1.20 will serve four or five more than adequately. We also recommend the hot pickle and sliced pork soup, 80 cents, for those who have a palate for the spicy. For those dining alone there is a small portion of most of the soups at 50 cents. The seven dumpling dishes which follow are among the best the authors have encountered. We especially endorse the pancake with green onion 50 cents, a hearty combination of browned dough and scallions measuring about 9 inches in diameter. The meat dumplings either steamed $1.00, fried $1.20, or boiled $1.00, are all excellent.

The cold dishes, a side of Chinese cooking not well known in New York, are very tasty. The jellyfish with sliced chicken $1.80 and the sesame sauce cold noodles are worthwhile extravagances. The rest of the menu is so large that it presents a happy fielder's choice.

A superb specialty for two is the crisp chicken (Tien Chin style) $3.00. The proprietors claim that chicken requires a week of marination before it is ready for cooking. It is then coated in a light batter and fried. It is served with fried salt and chili pepper. The char jan mein (with anzoutice meat sauce) is a big bowl of Chinese spaghetti garnished with an attractive arrangement of bean sprouts, cucumber and the mixed meat sauce—a fantastic bargain at 80 cents. Another featured dish is the moo-sui-pork $1.80. Moo-sui comes to the table in two parts. One is a mixture of slivered pork, vegetables and shredded egg and the other is the thin pancakes which cost an additional 10 cents each. An order of 4 to 6 should suffice for two people. The pork mixture is spooned into the pancake, rolled together and eaten by hand. The waiter will be pleased to demonstrate the entire technique.

Under the heading of casseroles are three outstanding dishes: mixed vegetable $3.00, fishhead $3.00, beancake $2.20. These dishes are elaborately prepared combinations of many ingredients which are cooked in a rich bubbling broth. It is brought to the table in an attractive deep clay bowl. Any of these casserole dishes can well serve three people and should not be missed.

The random recommendations include sliced pork with hot pepper $1.60, pork tenderloin broth garlic chili $1.80, sliced beef with bean preserve $1.60, sweet and sour bok choy $1.00, sweet and sour sea bass $2.50. The portions in most cases are liberal. A pleasant tea served in glasses which are filled as needed accompanies the meal.

The Dumpling House deserves the popularity it now enjoys but as a consequence the service suffers. Wilson Chang, the young proprietor along with his brothers are endlessly genial and try their best to make customers comfortable at all times.

Telephone:	MO 6-0160
Days Open:	6 days (Closed Saturday)
Hours Open:	8 A.M. to 8:30 P.M.
Bar:	No
Air Conditioning:	Yes
Recommended for:	Lunch. Dinner. Dating.
Your Comments:	
Food:	Fair to Good
Ambiance:	Fair to Good
Hygiene:	Good
Service:	Good

Vic and Katie's Fairmont Viennese Restaurant, at 116th Street and Amsterdam Avenue, MO-6-0160 is across the street from the Columbia University complex from which it draws most of its customers. In order to reach this little below-street-level restaurant from Broadway one has to cross the Columbia campus.

Katie, one of the restaurant's proprietors, runs the scene with energetic concern. Her attempt is to combine the old-world cooking tradition with contemporary collegiate attitudes, tastes and budgets. The menu departs enough from Viennese dishes to give a reasonably broad cosmopolitan choice. To accommodate the students, the prices are properly low. On Friday evening, when students' energy is ebbing, Katie rebuilds the spirits of her wards by offering a double portion of any dish at no extra charge. There is a sandwich lunch in addition to main dishes. This offers a choice of soup or dessert, a sandwich and a beverage for 85 cents. Hero luncheons include bratwurst, veal cutlet, steak, meatballs (heroes, naturally, with either coffee or a soda) for 95 cents. The same dishes available on the dinner menu are there for the choosing; without soup or dessert they are 35 cents less than the stated price. The same offer prevails at dinner, but the full-course affair is recommended as a good buy. As a starter there is a choice of soup or juice. A good-sized bowl of home-made soup is served. The lentil soup is a healthy dish (35 cents à la carte) and, taken with a dessert, could very well make a satisfactory meal. The entrées range from fundamental student-stuffers to dishes that give more play to the sensitive Viennese hand. The bill of fare includes spaghetti with meat sauce ($1.40); meat ravioli ($1.55); bratwurst with sauerkraut ($1.75) (authors' choice); manicotti ($1.85); stuffed green peppers, a tasty *mittel*-European staple ($1.85)—(an authors' choice). Calves' brains, beurre noir, breaded mushrooms with tartar sauce, roast chicken, broiled liver and filet of sole are all in the $1.95 class. Delights such as boneless short ribs of beef and the classic Wiener schnitzel are $2.35 and $2.40 respectively. When it comes to the desserts, Viennese will be Viennese and the patrons are the fortunate beneficiaries. There is a choice of chocolate cake, strawberry shortcake (this is served as a deep-dish cake), rum cake or rum ball, all of which are home-made. If you are driven by an expensive sweet tooth,

15 cents more will permit you to indulge yourself in a Sachertorte, or strudel, apple or cherry.

The portions are generous. Add a full basket of bread with butter and a dish of cole slaw to any of these meals, and no one should leave the Fairmont Viennese hungry. Coffee in the appropriate Austrian spirit is excellent.

The dining room is the basement of an apartment house and is of modest size. It is brightly lighted, neat, but tight for space. There is a studied attempt to keep the room appealing, although the decor is made up largely of pseudo-antique kitchen objects and ordinary engravings.

An interesting feature is the daily tea hour that extends from 2 to 5 P.M. except Saturday, when the restaurant is closed. Cake is served with your beverage for a total cost of 40–50 cents. If you want a touch of old Vienna, the Viennese coffee at 35 cents will do the trick. Service by the waitresses has a pleasant maternal quality about it and is professionally prompt.

The food at the Fairmont Viennese is more solid than unusual, but it provides a distinct culinary bonus for the Columbia University neighborhood.

Telephone: None

Days Open: 6 days (Closed Sunday)

Hours Open: 11:30 A.M. to 7 P.M.

Bar: No

Air Conditioning: Yes

Recommended for: Lunch. Dinner. Dating?

Your Comments:

Food: Good

Ambiance: Fair

Hygiene: Fair

Service: Fair

The Foccaceria, 195 First Avenue, is a unique institution in Manhattan. Its principal offering is vestada, a bizarre Sicilian sandwich. At the entrance of this small restaurant there are two flat pans filled with steaming water. Floating in one are strange, thin white rectangles and in the other strange, thin gray rectangles. The white objects turn out to be boiled ricotta cheese; the gray, calves' spleen. The latter, an organ meat also called milt, is found in old-world Jewish cooking, where it is combined with lung to form a very hearty stew. To make a vestade, the proprietor opens a sliced sesame-seeded Italian bun, inserts a layer of ricotta, a layer of spleen and tops the two with shavings of Parmesan cheese. To partake of this southern Italian delicacy may seem to require something bordering on courage, but in point of fact the sandwich is unexpectedly mild and quite tasty. The price of a vestade is 30 cents, and two make a very adequate lunch. The rest of the limited and unwritten menu includes tripe, prepared both as a soup and as a stew, an authors' choice, at 75 cents. Both versions are skillfully and tastefully made. On Friday the specialty of the house is spaghetti with sardines. This is a basic dish in Calabria and Sicily but rarely found in New York. As a pasta variation, this dish makes a worthwhile addition to any spaghetti eater's repertoire. The menu changes from day to day, and it is best to ask for the daily special. The service as well as the restaurant is unadorned.

Telephone:	MU 4-8875
Days Open:	6 days (Closed Sunday)
Hours Open:	M. through Th., 6 P.M. to 10 P.M.; F., Sat., 6 P.M. to 11:30 P.M.
Bar:	No
Air Conditioning:	No (Garden)
Recommended for:	Dinner. Dating.
Your Comments:	
Food:	Fair to Good
Ambiance:	Good
Hygiene:	Fair to Good
Service:	Fair

Gloria's, 134 E. 26th Street just east of Lexington Avenue, is a small, subterranean, red-tablecloth, candlelit restaurant. It has that nostalgic appearance of the kind of hideaway seen in a 1937 movie in which Joel McCrea proposes to Teresa Wright. As the menu advises, all the main dishes are prepared to order, but this is a mixed blessing. The average wait for an order seems about 30 minutes. The habitués come prepared with a bottle of wine, which is brought in from the outside. The management encourages this practice, and there is a liquor store conveniently located a block away on East 27th Street.

The food itself is either Italianized American or Americanized Italian in style. The menu presents a fairly varied choice but contains few surprises. In fact the only unexpected dish is the calves' liver à la maison—small slices of liver sautéed with onions and mushroom in a thin wine sauce. It was rather tasty and an authors' choice at $1.85. Other dishes on the menu include London broil ($1.85), lasagna ($1.50), manicotti ($1.65), veal and peppers ($1.85) and eggplant parmigiana ($1.40). All the main courses are served with a small dish of spaghettini or a vegetable. Spaghetti dishes range from $1.25 to $1.80, depending on the sauce.

Italian bread comes with the meal, and the menu lists pizza bread and garlic bread at 50 and 35 cents respectively. When available, the big bargain among the desserts is zuppa Inglese at 40 cents, which is the lowest price the authors have found for this rich whipped egg confection. The other desserts run to the standard tortoni and spumoni. Espresso is available at 30 cents, and the American coffee at 15 cents was only fair. Though the food at Gloria's is not extraordinary, the atmosphere is comfortable, modest and romantic enough to provide a pleasant evening.

Telephone:	864-9106
Days Open:	6 days (Closed Sunday)
Hours Open:	11:30 A.M. to 9 P.M.
Bar:	No
Air Conditioning:	Yes
Recommended for:	Lunch. Dinner. Dating?
Your Comments:	
Food:	Good
Ambiance:	Fair
Hygiene:	Good
Service:	Good

The Green Tree, 1034 Amsterdam Avenue (at 111th Street), is another of the culinary benefits New York received from the influx of Hungarians during the late Fifties. This Hungarian-American restaurant occupies a corner virtually within the Columbia University campus. It has fed enough undergraduates in its nine years of existence to qualify its substantial dishes as part of the college curriculum. There are very few restaurants in this city that recognize the special budgetary problems a college student has when feeding himself. Mr. and Mrs. Kende, the proprietors of the Green Tree, operating along the lines of the traditionally European student-restaurant, have scaled the prices of their dishes to fit their clients' pockets. They have carried out this noble effort without any sacrifice of quality or quantity and, what is more, without any lessening of the proper restaurant amenities.

Though Columbia students constitute the bulk of the Green Tree trade, the restaurant is conducted along traditional lines so that any non-student diner would feel perfectly comfortable at any time.

The student lunch offered every day from 11:30 A.M. to 3:00 P.M. (10 percent discount for a weekly meal ticket) is a genuine bargain. It offers Hungarian goulash at 99 cents à la cart (sic), a well-cooked stew of tender beef in an unmistakably paprika-flavored sauce (an authors' choice); chicken paprikash (99 cents), similar to the goulash but with chicken as the basic meat and of course the ever-present national spice, paprika; stuffed or szekely cabbage (85 cents), ground beef with rice rolled within a cabbage leaf cooked in a delicious sauce; chopped steak à la Budapest (90 cents), a well-flavored and highly garlic-scented ground-beef preparation; stuffed pepper (85 cents), another combination spiced ground-beef and rice filling for a green pepper stewed all together in a rich sauce; and finally brains with eggs (95 cents), an unusual combination for Americans, but when cooked in beurre noir (browned butter) it makes a very palatable dish. All these entrées and many others are available on the dinner menu at a higher price. For example the goulash is $1.55 at dinner. Equivalent increases prevail for the other dishes. On the made-to-order menu (the restaurant warns of a

20-minute wait) there are many interesting dishes, such as breaded liver ($1.65), chicken liver à la Budapest ($1.75), brook trout ($1.75), hot pastrami plate ($1.65) and broiled rib steak ($1.95), among others. For both the luncheon and dinner menus an additional 50 cents will get you appetizer, dessert and a beverage as well. Among the appetizers the authors chose a cauliflower soup, made with fresh cauliflower and other vegetables, it was a solid but sensitively cooked dish.

On the à la carte menu the soup is 35 cents. You may have borsht or marinated herring or chicken liver as well as fruit or fruit juices. The two delicious home-made desserts are the palacsinta (described on page 103) and apple strudel. The palacsinta (authors' choice), 35 cents à la carte, consists of two crêpes, one filled with cheese and the other with an orange jam gently sprinkled with powdered sugar. A lunch confined to just soup and palacsinta is more than adequate. The pies are good but are of the sort that are commercially available. Sandwiches are from 35 to 50 cents, including a cheese-omelet version, hot pastrami and the college standby, the cheeseburger. Four omelets—western ($1.00), cheese (85 cents), brains ($1.00) and ham ($1.00)—round out the heavy end of the bill of fare. The coffee, obviously brewed to help students with their late-evening studies, is strong and costs 15 cents. Cognizant also of the energy needs of the student body, the Green Tree provides truly formidable portions. Most dishes, whether on the lunch or the dinner menu, come practically besieged by a huge array of home-made Hungarian noodles (nockerl), rice, potatoes, cauliflower and peas.

The room is squarish, clean and tidy, and each table has neatly arranged silverware on a white paper place mat, as well as a vase of artificial flowers. The decor is left to a group of circular framed mirrors and a few chromos.

The service reflects the parental concern that such a restaurant must have for its wards. It is interested, homey and prompt. The Green Tree is a simple restaurant and the cooking is basic, with a quality quite high for the price and the portions exceptional.

Telephone: 473-9805

Days Open: 7 days

Hours Open: 7 A.M. to 10 P.M.

Bar: No

Air Conditioning: Yes

Recommended for: Breakfast. Lunch. Dinner. Dating.

Your Comments:

Food: Good

Ambiance: Excellent

Hygiene: Excellent

Service: Good

Hammer's Dairy Restaurant, 243 E. 14th Street (near Second Avenue), is and has been an institution on that changing street for over 50 years. This eating establishment is an almost perfect physical preservation of a restaurant of the Thirties. With the exception of the formica rather than the milk-glass table tops, all details of decor are remarkably consistent. From the gold-leaf script on the window and the gold-white stucco walls to the heavily shellacked wooden dividers between table rows the total effect is as though one had stepped back into time. Hammer's is what it has always been: an immaculately clean, wonderfully lit (artificial and daylight), unpretentious, comfortable restaurant.

The development of Jewish dairy cuisine is treated in some detail on page 22, and what is said there applies generally to Hammer's. However, Hammer's is a genuine restaurant rather than a luncheonette. Its copious bill of fare offers about five times as many choices as the much smaller B & H. There are 7 soups, 20 salad choices, 16 egg and omelet offerings, 5 ways of serving potatoes, 11 sour cream dishes, 20 appetizers, 8 fish entrées, 21 meats, 11 vegetables dishes, 19 desserts and a section of 5 international specialties. These dishes somehow evade classification. A sample listing is perhaps the best description:

Asparagus tips on toast, vegetable, potato ($1.30), Vegetarian chop suey with mushroom ($1.45), Cauliflower à la king, garden peas, potato ($1.35), Eggplant steak parmigiana, vegetable ($1.50), French toast, syrup and jam ($.85).

Despite the magnitude of the menu, Hammer's maintains a high quality for each of its dishes. As a starter try the schav for 70 cents (authors' choice), a sort of Jewish vichysoisse made of sour grass thick with fresh sour cream. A healthy boiled potato may be added for another 15 cents. Farmer's-style potato soup (55 cents) is another filler. In the main, the appetizer selections seem to be high-priced. Worthy dishes include smoked salmon and cream cheese ($1.40), imported sprats and trimmings ($1.20), smoked whitefish ($1.50). A traditional way of getting around the expensive appetizer is to partake liberally from the constantly replenished cornucopia of bread, rolls and butter that accompany the meal. Fish preparation in the Jewish manner provides some pleasant surprises. Some examples are pickled fish (undetermined species) served with lettuce and tomato, for $1.75, fried herring with onions and vegetable ($1.20), cold boiled carp or pike with chilled gravy (fish jelly) for $1.75 and smoked sable carp ($1.50). The roast list contains the usual amusing transmutations, such as baked vegetarian lamb chop ($1.30) and protose steak ($1.40). An authors' choice is the potato noodles with fried onions and semelbrezel (a good-sized mound of thick noodle fingers covered with sweet browned onions and the mysterious semelbrezel) for $1.10. Other good buys are the potato pancakes with apple sauce and sour cream ($1.25), apple or banana fritter served with jam or syrup ($1.10). Also under dairy dishes are matzoh brie ($1.30) and mamaliga. The former is described on page 22 and the latter is merely a firm corn-meal mush served with farmer's cheese and butter. Fried cheese kreplach and cream ($1.25) is also worth a try. Among the many egg dishes the smoked salmon (lox) omelet for $1.25 is a happy combination.

Fruit lovers can find an ample assortment among the desserts. There are melons in season (45 cents), baked apple with or without cream (40 cents), stewed prunes (35 cents), apple sauce (30 cents). Those without concern for calories may try the special cheese cake (40 cents), apple strudel (30 cents), noodle charlotte—a baked lattice of noodles, cheese and raisins—banana shortcake (50 cents). Coffee, never a Jewish culinary triumph, is not bad at Hammer's. Service can vary but it is generally pleasant and is remarkably quick.

It is one of the few inexpensive restaurants which offer fine food in a compatible environment.

Telephone:	MO 6-3450
Days Open:	7 days
Hours Open:	11:30 A.M. to 11 P.M.
Bar:	Yes
Air Conditioning:	Yes
Recommended for:	Lunch. Dinner. Dating.
Your Comments:	
Food:	Good to Excellent
Ambiance:	Good
Hygiene:	Good
Service:	Fair to Good

The Harbin Inn is a large, professionally run Shanghai and Peking-style restaurant located at 2637 Broadway, (100th Street) on the upper West Side. It is one of the authors' unprovable laws that a good Chinese restaurant can be determined by the character of its clientele. The proper mix is 30 percent professional types, 20 percent alert-looking college students, 25 percent from the arts, 15 percent Chinese, and a 10 percent sprinkling of the miscellaneous. This is just about what you'll find at the Harbin Inn. The decor of this restaurant gives the appearance of a much more expensive establishment.

The six-page menu lists an amazing 170 separate Shanghai and Peking dishes that provide a field day for the adventurous eater. Even the cognoscenti will find many unfamiliar and attractive items. Those content to remain on more familiar ground will find a comfortable selection from the two pages of conventional Cantonese dinners.

Some of the dishes that have special appeal for the authors are the Harbin soup: fishballs, spinach, black mushrooms and jellied noodles in a thin broth (80 cents for two); Family's bean cake, a mixture of fried slices of bean curd, pork with scallions and bamboo shoots steeped in a fiery, burnt-sienna-colored sauce ($1.50); and a delicately steamed sea bass cooked with black beans and slices of ginger called, appropriately enough, steamed fish with black bean sauce ($1.75).

Other interesting choices include chicken with cashew nuts ($2.00), Chinese sausage with vegetable ($1.65), mou sui pork with pancakes ($1.85), sliced abalone sauté ($1.75), and noodles with smoked fish ($1.25). The fish dishes at Harbin are particularly well prepared. In every case the portions are large and attractively presented. Desserts are a cut below the inventive main-dish menu and follow the routine patterns of most Chinese restaurants. Service is prompt and efficient enough, but just a bit aloof.

SEE ERRATA, page 5

HELLENIC PALACE

Telephone: 246-5266 and 586-9430

Days Open: 7 days

Hours Open: 11 A.M. to 1 A.M.

Bar: Yes

Air Conditioning: Yes

Recommended for: Lunch. Dinner. Dating.

Your Comments:

Food: Excellent

Ambiance: Good to Excellent

Hygiene: Excellent

Service: Good

The Hellenic Palace, 141 W. 47th Street, is a sparkling clean, exuberantly decorated Greek restaurant bounded on the east by Manhattan's throbbing jewelry district and on the west by Times Square. The blue-and-white decor and the high quality of the food suggest a considerably more expensive restaurant. The Kletsidis family all work in the operation of the restaurant. Chris Kletsidis, the father, was a noted chef in Athens and does virtually all the cooking with an occasional hand from his wife. Teddy, the son, functions as manager and maître d'hôtel with rare concern and amiability. The authors consider the food at the Hellenic Palace some of the best among any of the Greek restaurants in New York. The luncheons offer a choice of 10 dishes: eggplant moussaka for $1.35 (authors' choice); Greek cheese omelet ($1.45), unusually good; oriental baked macaroni ($1.35); charcoal-broiled shish kebab ($1.75). The entrée price includes dessert and a beverage. Add 10 cents more for Greek coffee. For dessert the galactoboureko, a mild pudding with honey, is truly delectable, as is the unusually light baklava.

The dinner is à la carte but replete with inexpensive and excellent dishes. The fine Kletsidis touch is obvious in its seafood. The sea bass ($1.75) or porgy ($1.50) is served with avgolemono, the basic Greek sauce of egg and lemon. The Athenian treats are the djajak, a robust combination of cut cucumbers, spices and garlic (80 cents); and a taramosalata, a suave mixture of red caviar and cheese (85 cents). One can also find on the menu such delightful items as gold spinach and cheese pie ($1.25), calf's brains sautéed ($1.85), and the ever-present stuffed vine leaves ($1.00).

The service is always pleasant and reasonably prompt. The dishes are brought to the table on wooden serving platters. All the food looks very attractive. The Hellenic Palace is licensed to serve beer and wine. Fix, a first-rate Greek beer is available in bottles, along with other American brands. Because of its convenient midtown location, truly fine food and pleasant surroundings, the Hellenic Palace is a standout.

Telephone:	WO 2-9588
Days Open:	7 days
Hours Open:	24 hours
Bar:	No
Air Conditioning:	Yes
Recommended for:	Lunch. Dinner. Dating.
Your Comments:	
Food:	Good to Excellent
Ambiance:	Fair
Hygiene:	Fair
Service:	Poor to Fair

Hong Fat, 63 Mott Street, is one of the multitudinous restaurants on Chinatown's main street. It has been the gastronomic mainstay of many artists and students because of its excellent noodle (mein) dishes, which may be had at very reasonable prices. This combination of virtues, price and quality is responsible for packing the long main room at almost any hour of the day. Chinese noodles are a gastronomic invention of great variety. Hong Fat is one of the few restaurants that exploits the full range of noodle preparation.

Before one gets into an elaborate choice of noodle dishes, there is a selection of 12 pleasant soups ranging from 30 cents to 90 cents. Some of these soups, especially the yat gaw mein (noodle and broth mixture with pork, chicken or beef), are quite filling. The four noodle categories are lo mein (soft noodles), special noodles with gravy, chow mai fon (fried rice noodles), chow fon (broad noodles). Within the categories are the tasteful permutations of chicken, pork, beef, fish, duck, shrimp, etc. Though the choice is not easy, some of our favorites are roast duck lo mein ($1.00) roast pork lo mein (75 cents), noodles with chicken and oyster sauce ($1.00), special noodles with shrimp and oyster sauce ($1.40), fish chow mai fon ($1.20), roast duck chow mai fon ($1.10), beef chow fon (85 cents). In addition to this solid list, Hong Fat offers a selection of interesting non-noodle mixtures: clams Chinese style ($1.75), crab Chinese style ($2.00), snails Chinese style ($1.75). These dishes are heavily spiced with garlic. A select dish which is more than adequate for three to four people is whole chicken three ways for $5.00.

Service is on the rough side but quick. Tea is served in glasses which are refilled by the waiter throughout the meal. The spirit of Hong Fat is best expressed by this verbatim quote from its menu:

"*Please give your entire order at the same time because in the real Chinese style we serve everything together. All our Chinese food is delicious. The price is reasonable. No order ekchanged (sic) after it is prepared. Not responsibe (sic) for any personal property lost.*"

Hye Middle Eastern

Telephone:	MU 3-2555
Days Open:	Tuesday through Friday
Hours Open:	11 A.M. to 7 P.M.
Bar:	No
Air Conditioning:	No
Recommended for:	Lunch.
Your Comments:	
Food:	Good
Ambiance:	Fair
Hygiene:	Good
Service:	Fair

The Hye Middle Eastern Food Shop, 539 Second Avenue (at 30th Street), MU 3-2555 advertises "a ready meal for all occasions—less work for ladies." B. Khanjian, the wiry and intense proprietor, is probably the world's greatest Oriental finger snapper (ask for a demonstration). The food shop is an Armenian grocery dealing principally in canned and packaged Oriental foods. These include such staples and delicacies as fava beans, walnuts rolled in grape-juice paste, sesame pastel candy bars, braided and unbraided feta cheese, stuffed grape leaves, thin Armenian bread, Middle Eastern pastries and dried rolled apricot sheets. The primary reason for the store being included in the *Underground Gourmet* is that it offers lahmajin, also known as Oriental pizza. Quite simply, these are thin, eight-inch-diameter tasty, crisply baked, unleavened dough disks covered with chopped meat, fresh tomatoes, parsley and spices. The pizza is folded into thirds, wrapped in paper and served hot. Its flavor is lighter and subtler than the common Italian pizza. Two or three lahmajin would make a light, if one-dimensional, lunch. The pizzas are 35 cents each, two for 60 cents, five for $1.35 and ten for $2.45. Mr. Khanjian's menu also features a small, changing and random assortment of Middle Eastern items: grape leaves are 85 cents, eggplant 85 cents, stuffed cabbage 90 cents, hommos tahini 70 cents (described on page 40), fava beans 65 cents and a choice of Oriental pastry at 25 cents each. Sodas go well with pizza, and Armenian coffee is best with the pastry. The room is essentially a store with a long counter and a few stools. Besides the canned merchandise on the walls the take-out foods are displayed in a glass refrigerator case at the rear of the store. Overhead, Japanese lanterns complete the decor. Don't forget to ask Mr. Khanjian to give that demonstration of finger snapping.

Telephone: RH 4-9685

Days Open: 7 days

Hours Open: 7 A.M. to 1 A.M.

Bar: Beer only

Air Conditioning: Yes

Recommended for: Breakfast. Lunch. Dinner. Dating?

Your Comments:

Food: Fair to Good

Ambiance: Fair

Hygiene: Fair

Service: Good

The Ideal Lunch and Bar, 238 E. 86th Street (between Second and Third avenues), forty years on Yorkville's main street, offers an extensive menu of solid German fare at workingman's prices. It is a long, high-ceilinged, drab-brown room with a counter running the length of the interior and a quite unexpected small balcony with seven tables at the rear. Most of the regular clientele is German and composed of working people and residents of the neighborhood who seem to be serious eaters. True to the German cooking tradition, the Ideal deals in sturdy food and a menu unfamiliar outside of Yorkville. There is always a daily soup special, and two soups the authors particularly commend to your attention are barley-vegetable and lentil at 30 cents each. An unusual treat is the suelze at 40 cents, a home-made head cheese (bits of meat in aspic) or galantine if one prefers a more elegant name. Twenty-five of the thirty-one main dishes feature some variation of meat. The range extends from the seldom-found saure kalbs herzen (sour calf's heart) with spinach and noodles ($1.10), pig's knuckles, sauerkraut and potatoes $1.20, Koenigsberger klops (beef patties) with caper sauce and vegetables ($1.10), to the more familiar boiled beef with horseradish sauce ($1.40) or Yankee pot roast and red cabbage ($1.40). Somewhere in between there is a tasty smoked pork tenderloin, sauerkraut and potato for $1.40. For a dish somewhat outside the American palate one can try the liver dumplings, sauerkraut and potatoes at $1.10. As one might expect, the bratwurst and knockwurst with potato salad or sauerkraut are terrific. The German pancake, an eight-inch-diameter heavyweight crêpe served with applesauce, is an excellent buy at 85 cents.

Desserts are uninspired, but one will hardly miss them after a session with the formidable portions which the Ideal serves. A marvelous selection of imported German beers, including Dinkelacker, Würzburger and Löwenbraü, is available at 60 cents. A glass of house draft beer, which goes very well with this sort of food, is 20 cents. The rye bread is disappointing.

German food suffers, as a rule, from prolonged cooking. The Ideal is in this culinary mold, but the wholesome ingredients used, the heavily burdened plates, and the indefatigable service make it a worthwhile find.

SEE ERRATA, page 5

Telephone:	GR 7-9628
Days Open:	6 days (Closed Sunday)
Hours Open:	M. through F., 5 P.M. to 9:30 P.M.; Sat., 5 P.M. to 10 P.M.
Bar:	Yes
Air Conditioning:	Yes Garden
Recommended for:	Dinner. Dating.
Your Comments:	
Food:	Fair to Good
Ambiance:	Fair to Good
Hygiene:	Fair to Good
Service:	Fair to Good

Il Faro, 229 E. 14th Street, is the kind of restaurant that used to abound in New York about 15 to 20 years ago—a restaurant that was family-owned, unpretentious, frequented by students, artists, radicals, working people, all who were attracted by its informal atmosphere and substantial food. Most of these restaurants have vanished or have changed their character, but Il Faro has held onto many of the virtues of its humble earlier period. The restaurant is a long, extremely narrow, high, tin-ceilinged room with a spirit of a meeting place about it. There are two rows of white-tablecloth-topped tables that hug the side walls. Both in its service and cooking the style of Il Faro is straightforward and reliable. The plates are heavy, stenciled china, the wine comes in water tumblers and the tomato sauce is always thick, bright red and homelike. Despite this essential working-class orientation, there are gourmet aspirations in many dishes. Indeed there is a special section of the menu surprisingly devoted to "French entrées": escargots de bourgogne (6 snails) at $1.00; rognons sauce maderire (sic)—veal kidneys ($1.95); escalopes de veau à la creme and salad ($1.85); riz de veau sauce bechamelle (sic)—sweetbreads—($2.10); and duck à l'orange ($1.60). The cooking, however, is most convincing in its repertoire of Italian (mostly southern) dishes. There are several enjoyable ways to begin a meal; for example: green soup (escarole in broth) at 45 cents, a light and flavorful dish and an authors' choice. The red beans and macaroni soup is substantial enough to take the edge off a fierce appetite—45 cents. Baked clams oreganate, six for $1.00, and pimientos and anchovies at 50 cents are two more pleasant starters. In the farinaceous (pasta) section, spaghetti, linguine, ziti and ravioli vary in price according to the sauce with which they are served: marinara ($1.15), shrimp ($1.75), meat (95 cents), meat ball ($1.20), anchovies (95 cents), sausages ($1.65). Finishing off the pasta choices are home-made lasagna ($1.35), baked manicotti ($1.00) and finally fettucine Alfredo ($1.55). Some of the less conventional dishes include shrimp sukoff (shrimps broiled in butter with a lemon sauce), a house specialty ($1.85), an authors' choice; veal kidney cacciatore ($1.75); eggplant cacciatore with mushrooms ($1.80); broiled home-made Italian sausages ($1.65); brains sautéed in butter ($1.50); veal cutlet topped with eggplant ($2.00), an authors' choice.

In addition the menu carries a full complement of chicken, pork, veal and fish dishes all under $2.00. All dishes are served with a choice of spaghetti or green salad. The home-style cooking of Il Faro cannot be described as delicate or subtle. Il Faro's old-fashioned attributes are to be found in the unexpected wide variety of dishes, its giant-sized portions and the simple quality of its surroundings. The service is adequate except when the restaurant is crowded. The choice of coffee may be either instant American or slow but real Italian espresso. We recommend the latter.

SEE ERRATA, page 5

Telephone:	None
Days Open:	6 days (Closed Monday)
Hours Open:	6 P.M. to 11 P.M.
Bar:	No
Air Conditioning:	Yes
Recommended for:	Lunch. Dinner. Dating?
Your Comments:	
Food:	Fair to Good
Ambiance:	Fair
Hygiene:	Fair
Service:	Fair

The India Pakistan Restaurant, 183 Lenox Avenue (between 119th and 120th streets), 864-9419 is one of a handful of Indian restaurants in New York. Three of the simplest and least expensive are in Harlem. It would be very difficult to beat the prices of the India Pakistan, which are scaled to meet the pocketbooks of the neighborhood. Because Harlem is a ghetto area, it is not always a comfortable place for tourists. This modest restaurant, snuggled down three steps in a brownstone, is situated on one of the more attractive streets in the neighborhood and presents an unforbidding aspect for first-time visitors. The proprietor, Mr. Hason Miah, has operated this plain, clean establishment in Harlem for about 20 years. His menu lists only nine dishes, all convincingly authentic curries. The prices are phenomenally low. Curry is served with either rice or rooty, the latter being a soft, fried, flat, unleavened Indian bread. Rooty (a house specialty) adds anywhere from 5 cents to 20 cents to your curry dish, but the price never exceeds $1.10. A listing of the complete menu follows:

Kima curry, rooty ($1.05) with rice ($1.00), Chicken curry, rooty ($1.05) with rice ($1.00), Beef curry, rooty ($1.05) with rice ($1.00), Lamb curry, rooty ($1.05) with rice ($.95), Vegetable curry, rooty ($1.00) with rice ($.90), Fish curry, rooty ($1.00) with rice ($.80), Shrimp curry, rooty ($1.10) with rice ($1.05), Giblet curry, rooty ($1.00) with rice ($.80), Liver and heart curry, rooty ($1.00) with rice ($.80), Sweet mango chutney ($.25), Holdwa ($.20), Green mango pickle ($.25), Lemon pickle ($.25).

The curries are tasty and not too hotly spiced. But if you have tolerance for hot foods, a supplementary order of lemon pickle (25 cents) will easily burn a hole in the roof of your mouth. The other relishes are sweet mango chutney for 25 cents (fairly hot), holdwa for 20 cents (pretty hot), and green mango pickle for 25 cents (*very* hot). The long narrow room is basically utilitarian, furnished in fundamental chromium and leatherette and a jukebox toward the front. Service too is basic and utilitarian but not at all unfriendly. Portions are not overly large, but with curry a small amount goes a long way. The menu lists only one dessert: ice cream. Coffee and tea are available.

KAMEHACHI SUSHI

Telephone: 245-9871 and 765-4737

Days Open: 6 days (Closed Sunday)

Hours Open: Noon to 12:30 A.M.

Bar: Yes

Air Conditioning: Yes

Recommended for: Lunch. Dinner. Dating.

Your Comments:

Food: Good to Excellent

Ambiance: Fair

Hygiene: Fair

Service: Fair

Kamehachi Sushi, 41 W. 46th Street, is a Japanese luncheonette with a convincingly authentic atmosphere. It is a long, awkwardly arranged room with both table and counter service. Sitting at the counter gives one the advantage of observing two extraordinarily skilled Japanese short-order cooks at work. One can watch these indefatigable men slicing raw fish, molding rice balls, rolling seaweed and performing all the multifold operations involved in the preparation of the 17 dishes on the menu. The decor of the Kamehachi is plain, but there are many visual delights in this restaurant. A slender glass showcase which runs the length of the counter is filled with greens, seaweed, fresh fish and bean curd all beautifully arranged with characteristic Japanese grace. All the prepared dishes in turn are served with equal care. Sushi, a popular dish and the authors' choice ($2.00), is an exquisite, colorful composition of vinegared rice balls topped with a variety of raw fish filets, some wrapped in thin seaweed. It is served in a terra-cotta-colored lacquered bowl. For those who are hesitant to try raw fish, the authors can assure them that the taste is extremely delicate, and not unlike that of the very best smoked sturgeon. Tempura ($2.00), a more familiar dish, an assortment of shrimp, striped bass and any vegetable deep-fried in a light batter, is excellent. A special section of the menu is devoted to the somewhat less familiar ochazuke dishes, which are combinations of rice with either fish, roe or seaweed prepared by pouring tea over the ingredients. The broth that results is rich and unusual. These ochazuke dishes are all priced at $1.25. Some other items on the menu include mari-sushi, rice-filled bean-curd pockets ($1.25); yakitori, Japanese-style shish kebab of chicken ($2.00). Kamehachi, like other Japanese restaurants, does not serve large portions. The full-bodied green tea that accompanies the meal is replenished frequently. Service is pleasant but is hampered by the bad arrangement of tables which makes dining quite uncomfortable. The shortage of staff does not help either. Despite these deficiencies, the appearance, freshness and exotic quality of food make Kamehachi a commendable eating place.

Telephone:	AL 4-2246
Days Open:	7 days
Hours Open:	M. through Th., 7 A.M. to 1 A.M.; F., 7 A.M. to 2 A.M.; Sat., 7 A.M. to 3 A.M.; Sun., 7 A.M. to 1 A.M.
Bar:	Beer only
Air Conditioning:	Yes
Recommended for:	Lunch. Dinner. Dating?
Your Comments:	
Food:	Good
Ambiance:	Fair
Hygiene:	Poor
Service:	Fair* (see text)

Katz's, 205 East Houston Street, is the largest, busiest, noisiest and sloppiest delicatessen in Manhattan and very possibly in the world. Once inside the enormous room, one is assailed by the assorted smells of spiced meats, sour pickles, steaming sauerkraut, frying potatoes and the shouts of orders, clinking dishes and the rumbling of the bus boys' carts that provide a sight-and-sound background to the thousands of hanging salamis and flowing hordes of customers. The scene is like a living Brueghel painting.

The operating procedure is to get your ticket at the entrance, given to you by an old Katz hand whose contemptuous mien is an indication of things to come. You then muscle your way up to the endless serving counter and try to make yourself heard. The object of your attempt at communication is one of Katz's imperious master carvers. Protected by a wall of preserved meats and pickled tomatoes, these declassed princes maintain an undeviating arrogance toward their hungry petitioners. If you ever want to see an example of raw contempt, just try asking for an extra-lean pastrami sandwich. The justification for all this humiliation is the best Jewish-style delicatessen sandwich extant. It is made on the traditional Jewish rye bread or a pseudo-French bread inexplicably called "club." Between the two slices is heaped an unbelievable quantity of meat of your choice. The range of choice includes hot corned beef, hot pastrami, hot brisket of beef and cold rolled beef, roast beef and tongue, all 85 cents each. Salami, bologna, liverwurst and garlic wurst are 60 cents. Chopped liver is 65 cents. Combinations of any type are 95 cents. Turkey is 90 cents but in combination with other meats is $1.00.

A platter of assorted meats served with bread and pickle is $1.40. A Jewish-style omelet (pancake form) made with corned beef, pastrami or tongue is $1.40. The side dishes of home-made cole slaw, home-made potato salad, Heinz baked beans and the largest portions of broadly cut, greasy but tasty French-fried potatoes are 20 cents. The classic beverage to accompany Katz's food is a large bottle of Dr. Brown's celery tonic, called Cel-Ray (15 cents), curiously refreshing; all other flavors are available. A glass of tea (10 cents) or a bottle of beer (30 cents) make excellent liquid accompaniments to any type of Katz meal. Katz's all-beef frankfurters are large, juicy and incomparable. Delicious warm sauerkraut and home-made mustard are available at a separate self-service counter where festooning may be done at will.

Katz's is no place for the timid. Eating comfortably in the huge L-shaped room is trying. The embarrassing struggle with the countermen can be minimized somewhat by choosing one of the side tables which are set aside for waiter service. Then one has to deal only with the waiter's arrogance.

Whether a great sandwich is worth this psychic trial is a question only the individual can answer for himself. The number of people at Katz's on any given day at almost any hour demonstrates the triumph of greed over pain. On Sunday the swirling scene becomes less like a Brueghel and more like Michelangelo's Last Judgment.

Telephone: 964-2410

Days Open: 7 days

Hours Open: 7 A.M. to 8:30 P.M.

Bar: No

Air Conditioning: Yes

Recommended for: Lunch. Dinner. Dating.

Your Comments:

Food: Good to Excellent

Ambiance: Good

Hygiene: Good

Service: Good

Koon Shing Bakery and Restaurant, 202 Canal Street, is a relative upstart compared with such a venerable institution as Nom Wah (see page 125). This little restaurant, specializing in dim sum, opened its doors in 1966. It is apparent immediately that the preparation and quality of the dumplings reflect the authority that comes only from long experience. The most impressive part of the menu is the offering of 48 dim sum varieties listed as "hors d'oeuvres." Since only ten items are described on the menu, one must trust to the good judgment of the waiter about the undescribed 38. The illustrated guide on pages 126-35 could also be useful at Koon Shing. Some unusual dumplings that we found at Koon Shing were "crab delight" (a steamed crescent dumpling filled with meat and vegetables), three for 50 cents; tan crescent (a pastry filled with diced chicken), 15 cents each; golden tart (a sweet dessert-like fluffy pastry with custard filling), 15 cents each. What may very well be New York's best luncheon buy is listed as the "Seven Star Platter." This is a selection of seven different and delectable dim sum, chosen for their variety of shape, texture and taste, all attractively arranged and served with tea. How the management can afford to sell this attractive dish for a dollar is a genuine Chinese puzzle. The right-hand side of the menu is composed principally of noodle dishes at comparatively low prices. Chicken, duck, shrimp and a mysterious item called "variety" lo mein (soft noodles) are $1.25. Fish lo mein is $1.00, and for 95 cents there is a roast pork and a beef version of the wide rice noodles. Chicken, roast duck and the ever mysterious "variety," $1.10; fish, $1.00. A large wor mein (soft noodles and mixed vegetables, meat or seafood in broth) is a dish large enough for two or three, priced at $2.75. A smaller edition is $1.75.

At the entrance of the Koon Shing is a large glass display counter with a bewildering assortment of Chinese biscuits, cookies, pastries and cakes. Visually, many of these items are extraordinarily beautiful, some with intricate embossing, others stamped with red Chinese calligraphy on their shiny surfaces. They range in appearance from delicate round puffs to ancient clay tablets. The management has conveniently identified each item with a description of the ingredients. Roast pork, winter melon, and soy bean are some of the unlikely fillings for these pastries, but somehow they all turn out to be sweet. Pastries may be eaten in the restaurant or taken out. Prices range from 20 cents for a modest flat cake to 40 cents for a thick filled bun.

The formica decor is ordinary, saved only by its newness. Service, pleasant enough, becomes spotty during the busiest hours.

Telephone: None

Days Open: 7 days

Hours Open: 5 A.M. to 9 P.M.

Bar: Yes

Air Conditioning: No

Recommended for: Lunch. Dinner. Dating.

Your Comments:

Food: Good

Ambiance: Good

Hygiene: Good

Service: Good

The L & H Restaurant and Bakery, 1588 Second Avenue, (between 82nd and 83rd streets), is the kind of enterprise that one used to encounter more frequently in New York some years ago. Despite creeping urban renewal, the Yorkville area is still a stronghold of the old-fashioned, home-style, good-value eating place, and the L & H falls into that category. It is a long, narrow store with milk-glass-topped tables on one side and a display counter filled with baked goods on the other. The walls and ceiling are decoratively corrugated tin (in need of paint) and the floor is a classic example of early-1900 tilework. The cooking has a simple, home-style German-Hungarian bent. One should not look for haute cuisine here, but the dishes are obviously prepared with care and the portions have a motherly generosity. A large bowl of celery soup (25 cents) is especially flavorful and is unusual in the abundance of fresh celery used in its making. Goulash, a neighborhood institution, was good at the L & H, at $1.20. It was rich, the noodles were firm and the meat was tender and of good quality. A dish of surprising excellence (authors' choice) is a formidable German pancake served with applesauce (95 cents). Twelve inches across and made with eggs, it will serve as lunch or dinner. The menu carries the traditional complement of items characteristic of the bakery-type restaurant, plus some ethnic specialties such as bauernwurst and sauerkraut (85 cents), fresh ham with sauerkraut ($1.35), salami and eggs (75 cents), cheese and jelly omelet (70 cents), breaded pork chops served with vegetables and potatoes (90 cents). The proximity of the bakery counter makes a very tempting display. The excellence of the fruit pies (20 cents), the L & H version of the sacher torte (30 cents), a rich chocolate roll filled with fruit conserve (30 cents) more than fills any vacancy left after the entrée.

Telephone: CA 6-9572	
Days Open: 6 days (Closed Wednesday)	
Hours Open: 11:30 A.M. to 10 P.M.	
Bar: Yes	
Air Conditioning: Yes	
Recommended for: Lunch. Dinner. Dating.	
Your Comments:	
Food: Good to Excellent	
Ambiance: Fair	
Hygiene: Fair	
Service: Good	

Lam Kee, 3 Catherine Street, outwardly is one of the least inviting restaurants in Chinatown. Perhaps "restaurant" is too grand a word for this modest, unaffected 20-seat bistro situated on the dark side of Chatham Square. Away from the neon-lit center of Chinatown, both the 50-foot Catherine Street and Lam Kee are easy to overlook. Bounded by an apartment house on one side and a Chinese barber shop on the other, Lam Kee, with only a portion of the window revealing its interior, is barely visible. The interior is brightened by overhead fluorescent lights intensifying the sheen of the blue corrugated plastic sheets fastened to the walls. A noisy and ineffectual air conditioner and stacks of Coca-Cola cases encumber the room. The daily specials are written in rather beautiful Chinese calligraphy on colored strips of paper which are posted at random about the room. As a *coup de grâce* to discourage American Chinese-food enthusiasts, the large sign above the door on the outside reads "Chop Suey and Chow Mein."

For non-Chinese-speaking people, dining at Lam Kee is an act of faith, for virtually no English is spoken. As in some chic Parisian bistros where the proprietors determine what its customers should eat, the English-speaking diner at Lam Kee is at the tender mercies of the owner-cook. Prices, though reasonable, remain a secret until the bill is rendered. The only control a diner may enjoy is to point at an attractive dish at another table and use it as a sample. Fortunately, not only are the dishes attractive but the cooking is unexpectedly refined. On our last visit the proprietor presented us with a delicious hot and sour soup laden with strips of bean curd, sliced pork and tiger-lily buds. This was followed by a dish of tender beef with snow peas in a light-brown oyster sauce and another treat of ⅛-inch thick, bite-size pork chops in a sweet and spicy tomato-based mixture. We have been similarly rewarded on other occasions. Tea accompanying the meal is served in glasses refilled from time to time by the attendant waiter. No individual dinner plates are put on the table, the assumption at Lam Kee being that you will eat in the Chinese manner, taking morsels from the serving dishes, combining them in your rice bowl and eating the two together. All this is best done with chopsticks and little concern for niceties. Lam Kee is a proletarian, neighborhood restaurant, a place where residents can gather for spirited and frequently loud discussions. It makes no attempt to solicit or encourage tourist trade. Gourmets must come here prepared to respect the customs of the house. There are risks, unknowns and some small discomforts in dining at Lam Kee. The authors believe these difficulties pale when compared with the excellent food that one finds there.

Telephone: 477-9633	
Days Open: 7 days	
Hours Open: 5 A.M. to 11 P.M.	
Bar: No	
Air Conditioning: Yes	
Recommended for: Lunch. Dinner. Dating?	
Your Comments:	
Food: Good to Excellent	
Ambiance: Fair	
Hygiene: Fair to Good	
Service: Fair to Good	

On the eastern fringe of the Slavic section lining Tompkins Square, at 111 Avenue A, where "New Bohemia" has taken root, there are several small Polish-Ukrainian restaurants that form Manhattan's "Pirogi Belt."

The pirogi, piroshki or pirogen is a dough pocket with a filling. It is roughly equivalent to the Italian ravioli, Chinese wonton, Jewish kreplach or Russian pelmeny. Leshko's like other member restaurants of this community, uses either sauerkraut, potato, cheese or meat for its unexcelled pirogi. An order of meat-filled pirogi (authors' choice) comes seven to the plate, swimming in butter, and costs 80 cents. It provides a most ample and satisfying dish. The Leshko bill of fare also includes such Ukrainian staples as cabbage soup, boiled beef, goulash and studenina, which is a rare and extraordinarily well-prepared dish of jellied pigs' feet. Desserts are ordinary and coffee is about diner quality.

The restaurant has a neutral decor, and the all-over feeling is clean and pleasant. There are a few small tables, but the bulk of eating is done at a large counter that runs the length of the room. Service is prompt, though the style and courtesy seem to vary with the server. The charming Mrs. Leshko, who attends the register, assured the authors that all dishes are freshly prepared every day. This restaurant is popular with the hipster as well as the entrenched Slavic community.

Telephone: WO 2-9085

Days Open: 7 days

Hours Open: 24 hours

Bar: No

Air Conditioning: Yes

Recommended for: Lunch. Dinner. Dating.

Your Comments:

Food: Good to Excellent

Ambiance: Fair to Good

Hygiene: Fair to Good

Service: Good

Lin's Garden, 53 Bayard Street, is one of the few restaurants open 24 hours a day. This is not a nominal accommodation, for frequently lines of night people are seen standing outside this small restaurant at two or three o'clock in the morning waiting for tables. The late-night (or early-morning) Chinatown eating foray is one of this city's great adventures. The cooking is Cantonese, a style not generally favored by the authors because it is the most common and the most abused. Lin's demonstrates, however, that with proper concern the Cantonese style can be very good indeed.

Noodle dishes represent one category of specialties, and they are offered in a wide range of preparations combined with soups, sauces, meats and vegetables. The yat gaw mein features noodles in soup and comes in four styles: with roast pork (60 cents), beef, chicken and roast duck (95 cents). These dishes are excellent and filling and could well serve as a complete light lunch. There are, in addition, ten other good soups ranging in price from 30 to 95 cents. The lo mein (soft noodles) are all good buys. They range from a low of 85 cents for roast pork to a high of $1.10 for the roast duck. Beef young sing chow fon ($1.60), one of the eight broad noodles (chow fon) dishes (authors' choice), an enormous mound of these noodles, bok choy mustard greens, sautéed beef in a whitish sauce is certainly enough to warm the insides of two solid eaters. The same dish with fine rice noodles (chow mai fon) is 10 cents more. These finer noodles, too, come in an assortment of flavors. The roast pork is 95 cents, vegetable 95 cents, beef $1.00. Under the special noodles (which are not unlike linguine) with gravy section, there are 14 varieties. One of the best is noodles with spareribs and black bean sauce, only 95 cents and an authors' choice. Others are noodles with chicken and oyster sauce ($1.00), curried noodles with pork (95 cents), and shrimp with curried noodles ($1.10). There are 16 similar dishes with a rice base within the same price range. In general, $1.00 goes a long way. Besides the noodle dishes, there are many other commendable entrées. In the seafood category, crab, clams and snails, Chinese-style, are all prepared in a unique way. They are steamed and drenched in a delicious thick sauce composed of eggs, ground pork and a heavy dose of garlic. Clams and snails are $1.75 and a huge dish of crabs $2.00. All are unqualified authors' choices. These dishes make for messy, cumbersome but rewarding eating. Under the "special dish" heading is a whole chicken three ways ($5.50). This dish consists first of a pleasant, pale, bland chicken soup with bean curd and vegetables, followed by an elegant dish of boned white meat combined with almonds, water chestnuts and mixed Chinese vegetables, and finally a dark, spicy sweet and sour mix of the remainder of the chicken—i.e. wings, neck, legs, with carrots, pineapple, peppers, tomatoes, etc. This dish serves four very nicely.

The menu is large, and in the other categories there are numerous dishes representing good value. Portions at Lin's are among the largest the authors have found in any Chinese restaurant. The family dinner at $2.20 per person offers a lot of food and an interesting choice of entrées.

Lin's Garden has only one dining room and it seats only 42. Recently decorated, the room is a sort of Chinese baroque of white and gold formica. During peak hours you will have to share your table with other diners. Service is fast, direct and efficient.

Telephone: 477-4460	
Days Open: 7 days	
Hours Open: 5 P.M. on	
Bar: No	
Air Conditioning: No	
Recommended for: Dinner. Dating.	
Your Comments:	
Food: Good to Excellent	
Ambiance: Good	
Hygiene: Fair to Good	
Service: Good	

The Little Kitchen, 242 E. 10th Street, just west of 1st Avenue
is one of the rare restaurants beyond the confines of Harlem
which serves "soul food." The term "soul food" refers to funda
mental Southern Negro cooking, the ingredients of which, though
modest, seem to have special powers and significance. The bound
aries that enclose "soul foods" are vague, but included in tha
mystical grouping are fried chicken, barbecued ribs, chitterling
(pronounced "chittlins"), pig's feet, oxtail, hot biscuits, yam
and collard greens. On page 151 we defined what we call
minimal restaurant. The Little Kitchen can be classified only a
subminimal. Princess Pamela, "your hostess," an attractive an
articulate woman, does all the shopping, preparation, cooking
sewing, dishwashing, bookkeeping and hostessing and very wel
indeed. The room is a typical neighborhood side street store
Pamela has decorated the room—which seats only 13—wit
Jewish memorial candles and various theatrical notices an
memorabilia posted at random. In matters culinary Pamela is
sensitive and authoritative cook. She is evasive about her recipe
and offers the claim that she cooks by feeling rather than b
measurement. Be that as it may, her fried chicken is the best th
authors have ever had. This dish, ordinarily a gastronomic cliché
in her hands becomes a very special treat. A large portion i
served, and it comes to the table glazed and crisp on the outside
tender and well cooked on the inside. The accompaniment con
sists of collard greens, which were prepared beautifully, withou
their customary bitterness, and black-eyed peas for $1.35 (author
choice). Oxtail, another inexpensive cut, was transformed into
tasty stew. This dish comes with collard greens and cold potat
salad, also $1.35. Both dishes were served with hot (great
home-made biscuits and crisp, fresh mixed salad of lettuce
tomatoes, scallions and cucumbers with a light oil, vinegar an
sugar dressing. For dessert there are fruit cobblers and home
made pies. Coffee is unusually good.

The menu changes from day to day, according to the marke

and Pamela's mood. The restaurant opens at 5 P.M. and closes at an indeterminate late hour. Various dishes run out at different times during the evening, and inevitably one has to take a sort of pot luck. Chances are you won't be unhappy.

Telephone:	RH 4-9508
Days Open:	7 days
Hours Open:	Noon to midnight
Bar:	No
Air Conditioning:	Yes
Recommended for:	Lunch. Dinner. Dating.
Your Comments:	
Food:	Good
Ambiance:	Good
Hygiene:	Good
Service:	Fair to Good

The Littleroyal Hungarian Restaurant, 1606 Second Avenue (between 83rd and 84th streets), is a small restaurant with a big menu. Few restaurants compete with this one in the number of spelling errors in its bill of fare, some of which can't help but be amusing. At any rate, the food at Littleroyal is very good. The menu is extensive and replete with unusual, exotic and rich dishes. One of the dishes on the appetizer list is roasted chicken liver (45 cents). Another is the gulyash soup (65 cents), one of the eight soups listed. Fruit soup and chicken soup Ujhazi-style, with a half chicken in it (really a main dish), are both first rate at $1.40. Gulyash, one of the pillars of Hungarian cooking, is served in four versions: beef, veal (authors' choice), pork or chicken, with noodles and salad for the surprisingly low price of $1.10. Gulyash, in point of fact a light delicate stew, has had its reputation sorely damaged by the abominations passed off under this label by luncheonettes and cafeterias. Littleroyal cooks it right. Chicken paprika, another mainstay, is $1.40. The less familiar side of this Hungarian menu includes heart and lung mix with bread dumpling for $1.20 (authors' choice), roast duck with fried potatoes and red cabbage for $1.60 (authors' choice), breaded chicken livers with home-fried potatoes and salad for $1.30, natural veal cutlet roasted with garlic for $1.60. A Viennese veal cutlet costs $1.40, and in the best-buy category there is a fried egg sausage and green mix for 80 cents. Instead of the potatoes one may have home-made noodles, spaetzel and nicely balanced sweet and sour cucumber salad. The wife of the owner does the cooking and she has a light, sensitive hand with the portions. In the critical area of dessert, where most cheap restaurants falter, the Littleroyal excels. Palacsinta (Hungarian crêpe) are delicious (55 cents), as is the gooseberry cream (50 cents), and the purée of chestnuts (60 cents) is rich beyond belief. There are five strudels: poppy seed, cherry, walnuts, cottage cheese and apple (35 cents). The Hungarians like noodles as a dessert, and there is a variety available, including noodle with apricot jam (50 cents). On the conservative side, there is melon and fruit in season (40 cents), or, at the other end of the spectrum, chocolate cake for 40 cents. In general the restaurant has a Continental feeling, and the voluminous owner seems to be on hand to keep things going when the service is lagging.

Telephone:	563-8081
Days Open:	7 days
Hours Open:	10 A.M. to 12:30 A.M.
Bar:	Yes
Air Conditioning:	Yes
Recommended for:	Lunch. Dinner.
Your Comments:	
Food:	Fair to Good
Ambiance:	Fair
Hygiene:	Poor to Fair
Service:	Good

The Maginas Tavern, 304 W. 40th Street, adjacent to the Port Authority Bus Terminal, reveals only a bustling bar from its street level. The restaurant division is one flight down. The Maginas is really a modest yet amply stocked cafeteria. The room itself, which seats 70, is on the seedy side, with a low ceiling, long banks of fluorescent lights, formica and leatherette furnishings and mirrored walls. At the rear are the kitchen and steam table with its huge open pots filled with authentically proletarian Greek food. Lamb, not unexpectedly, is the cornerstone of the bill of fare. In one form or another lamb is a component of 15 of the 30 listed entrées. Lamb kapama (a small shank) is tastily stewed with eggplant, string beans and okra, a good buy and an authors' choice at $1.35. Their lamb stew comes either with okra ($1.35) or unusual, bitter fibrous greens ($1.20). Large portions of these greens, served with olive oil, lemon or meat sauce, if you wish, are only 65 cents.

For those partial to meat roasts you may choose a roast loin of lamb ($1.65), leg of lamb ($1.50), shoulder of lamb ($1.50), leg of veal ($1.50), roast loin of pork ($1.50). All these dishes come with vegetables and/or rice. The latter is superbly done with an interesting touch of cinnamon.

A good beginning for any meal is the avgolemono soup (30 cents) or the more expensive taramosalata (70 cents), described on page 119. A filling, vegetarian-type meal can be made of the tomatoes stuffed with rice (90 cents) or the baked mixed vegetables (a Greek ratatouille) for 85 cents. For dessert, there is the conventional selection of Greek pastries, cheese and fresh fruit. The choice of domestic and imported beer is good, and a large glass of cold Rhoditys (a rosy, non-resinated dry wine) is 50 cents. Retsina for the hardier types is the same price. Greek coffee is 15 cents.

The countermen are robust, cheerful, helpful and willing to explain things to those unfamiliar with the Greek diet. The portions are properly sized to feed a Greek and principally masculine clientele. At lunchtime the room is lively, but in the evening the atmosphere takes on a somewhat quieter, even somber tone.

Telephone:	LO 3-4618
Days Open:	6 days (Closed Sunday)
Hours Open:	6:30 A.M. to 7:30 P.M.
Bar:	Just beer
Air Conditioning:	Yes
Recommended for:	Lunch. Dating?
Your Comments:	
Food:	Good
Ambiance:	Good
Hygiene:	Fair to Good
Service:	Fair

Manganaro's, 492 Ninth Avenue (between 37th and 38th streets), is located in the fascinating bazaarlike concentration of Greek and Italian food stores between Hell's Kitchen and Times Square. This large, bustling hero-parlor is the Italian counterpart of Katz's Delicatessen (see page 83). It is run by nine members of the Manganaro family: Mother and Father Manganaro, four brothers and assorted cousins and nephews. The Manganaros have been in the Italian import food business since 1873, and the hero-sandwich division is a nine-year-old offshoot. The eating establishment proper is a spacious store vigorously decorated in the red and green of the Italian flag. Its neo-pop quality is the product of the personal vision of gentle, philosophy-reading James Manganaro, one of the brothers.

Manganaro's really jumps from noon to about 1:30 P.M. Despite the healthy tumult, the service remains unusually courteous. The rush for lunch abates around 1:30, and relative calm prevails until closing at 7 P.M. A caution to post-rush-hour eaters—the supply of some foods tends to run out after the peak period, particularly the daily special.

The hero, basis of the Manganaro reputation, comes in a dizzying variety of choices. In addition to the 45 regular sandwiches, there are daily specials, such as tripe on Monday (85 cents); Tuesday and Thursday, pastrami (75 cents); Wednesday and Friday, squid (95 cents); and on Friday only, filet of cod (85 cents).

During this current hero-sandwich competition Manganaro's manages to stand apart by high quality and freshness of ingredients. Italian bread is delivered at three-hour intervals for the 1,000 heros prepared daily.

The desserts, largely commercially produced cakes and pastries, are undistinguished. The house-blended espresso, however, is rich and aromatic and a good buy at 20 cents. For those who occasionally are inclined toward a Continental breakfast, this is one of the few places where espresso or cappuccino is served from 6:30 A.M. on.

An unusual catering service offers a 6-foot hero stuffed with 12 meats and cheeses plus anchovies, sardines, peppers and sharply seasoned Italian vegetables, for $28.50. The management avers it will feed 25 people. There are 3-footers at $14.50, 4's at $19.50 and a 5-footer at $24.50 for those less ambitious.

The handsomely festooned adjoining store, also under Manganaro management, is one of the best places to shop for Italian delicacies.

Telephone:	JU 6-7340
Days Open:	Monday through Friday
Hours Open:	7 A.M. to 5 P.M.
Bar:	No
Air Conditioning:	Yes
Recommended for:	Breakfast. Lunch. Dating.
Your Comments:	
Food:	Excellent
Ambiance:	Good
Hygiene:	Excellent
Service:	Good to Excellent

Max's, 30 W. 47th Street, formerly of Antwerp and London, is a Jewish luncheonette cum restaurant. One comes upon this retreat in the lobby of an office building in the heart of the midtown jewelry district. The room is crowded, noisy with the sound of animated conversation, mostly about diamonds. The counter occupies most of the space, but there are several tables seating around 40 to 50 serious eaters. Decor is conventional luncheonette plastic and chrome. The over-all atmosphere is friendly, and Max, who is generally stationed at the register near the door, will greet you and see that you are seated comfortably. He and his wife, Irma, do all the cooking. He shops for and prepares the fish and meat dishes, while she does all the baking. Max's great specialties are his fish dishes: two kinds of gefülte fish, Polish, with sugar and the conventional without; pickled salmon-pike and, one day a week, boiled trout. We feel that the trout is extraordinary and is probably the best value of its kind at $1.25. There is also a wide array of meat and traditional dairy dishes. The daily change of fare is prominently displayed on a huge menu which covers a pillar at the rear of the dining room. Max and Irma are conscientious shoppers, and the ingredients are scrupulously fresh. The quality of the dishes reflects their continuing concern from purchase throughout preparation. In fact, this restaurant is one of the few places where fresh bay leaves are used. We especially recommend, in addition to the fish dishes, Friday's matzoh-ball soup with challah (egg bread with a twist) for 45 cents, frankfurter goulash, chicken, Russian egg salad and a full complement of sour-cream dishes. For dessert, either Irma's cheese cake or apple cake is excellent. Seltzer and matzohs are optional at no extra charge. Service is prompt and pleasant, with a pervasive feeling of harmony among the waitresses. Max and Irma Liptscher are both European Jews with a background of living in several countries. Max spent several years as a waiter and cook in Belgium and Irma lived in Fiume, Italy, for about 20 years. This has had the salutary effect of bringing lightness and sensitivity to traditional Jewish cooking, which has always suffered from a certain heaviness.

A sampling from the menu:

Lungen stew (stewed lung) ($.95), Hot calf's feet ($1.10), Frozen calf's feet ($.75), Boiled beef ($1.50), Klops with sholet (kishke) (stuffed intestine) ($1.10), Nova Scotia lox and cream cheese (on pumpernickel) ($.95), Sour cream with fruit (in season) ($.85).

Note: While Max's does not have a heavy breakfast trade, one can get such delights as an omelet, Jewish scrambled eggs and a good piece of herring. The peak lunch period from Monday through Friday is 12:30 to 1:30.

Telephone:	CA 8-2080
Days Open:	7 days
Hours Open:	Noon to 4 A.M.
Bar:	Yes
Air Conditioning:	Yes
Recommended for:	Lunch. Dinner. Dating.
Your Comments:	
Food:	Fair
Ambiance:	Excellent
Hygiene:	Fair
Service:	Fair to Good

Max's Kansas City, 213 Park Avenue South (at 18th Street), is within hearing distance of Union Square, New York's last outpost of vocal rebellion. Max's large neon sign and menu emphasize lobster, steak and chick-peas, but these items do not represent the full range of the restaurant's bill of fare. The restaurant is an enormous room—two floors, in point of fact—with a somewhat impermanent if not seedy quality about it. The tablecloths are a brilliant red, lending a strong accent to the surroundings. At the entrance, one encounters a crushed auto sculpture which sets an arty tone and creates a formidable traffic impediment. The walls are randomly decorated with large unconventionally shaped geometric canvases. The waitresses are young and generally shapely in their sweaters and mini skirts. The American-style food, served in ample portions, is good but not unusual. It is the ambiance of the place, a quality for which it rates high, which qualifies Max's Kansas City for this guide.

Like the unexplicable migration of the lemmings, a community of artists and hipsters has followed Max uptown from Greenwich Village, where he had operated a similar establishment. One reason may be the generous-sized drinks. As a result of Max's following, the restaurant is full of vitality, and interesting people.

The best food values are the special luncheons, which include soup, onion or tomato; entrée, chicken a la king ($1.25), baked meat loaf ($1.50), pot roast with pancake ($1.75). They are served with one vegetable and a very large salad that gives you a choice of dressings, including roquefort at no extra charge. A beverage is included too. The food is just serviceable, but you will not leave hungry. Some of the more interesting items on the à la carte menu are steak and eggs, vegetable or salad ($1.95); Max's beef and beer: prime sliced sirloin steak with a stein of imported beer ($2.25). Hot sandwich platters and salad plates ranging from $1.10 to $1.75 round out the menu. A nice and out-of-the-ordinary choice of domestic beers, Prior's dark and Mr. Sorley's ale, among others, are available at 50 cents.

The chick-peas are on every table. They are dry, hard, salty and kind of a drag. The menu also includes the following bit of folklore which we print in its entirety:

KANSAS CITY *consists of 121,901 people in Kansas, and 475,539 people in Missouri. It is famous as a way-station when jazz was traveling up the river, and, earlier, as a way-station when cows were traveling into beef. Geographically it is located quite near the center of the United States, and is part of the Mid-West. Sociologically it is part of the Bible-Belt. It is probably not a very good place to eat (the steaks went to New York), or listen (the music went to Chicago), or live (the people went to Los Angeles).* MAX'S KANSAS CITY *is named in sorrowful honor of this once-great metropolis, and here, in the middle of New York, one can once again spend evening after evening surrounded by the grandeur that was.*

Telephone: 874-8292 (Spanish-speaking)

Days Open: 7 days

Hours Open: Noon to midnight

Bar: No

Air Conditioning: Yes

Recommended for: Lunch. Dinner.

Your Comments:

Food: Good

Ambiance: Poor to Fair

Hygiene: Poor to Fair

Service: Poor

Mi Tierra, 668 Amsterdam Avenue (at 93rd Street), is a Mexican restaurant in a section of the upper West Side with a predominantly Spanish-speaking population. The difficulty and discomfort that one may encounter before getting around to eating the rather good food served at the Mi Tierra may be enough to discourage all but the most dedicated value seekers. The restaurant is a visual disaster. There are four scuffed plastic-covered tables which a total of 16. The wallpaper is a peeling simulated brick. Overhanging the entrance door is an enormous blue-painted air conditioner which originally must have been used for cooling a battleship. The counter, which seats 12, encloses the well-used and blackened open kitchen. The clientele, drawn principally from the neighborhood, is lively and discussions are carried on noisily. Frequently two or three very young children race through the restaurant or follow behind their mother as she waits on the table. Your order is taken promptly enough, but the length of time until the dish itself materializes before you is both inexplicable and interminable and, if you are very hungry, unendurable. The authors have averaged a 50-minute wait even when there was only one other customer in the restaurant. The reward turns out to be authentically prepared, tasty, quite well-arranged Mexican food at a reasonable price. The menu lists pork tacos and salad ($1.50), embuladas corn tortillas, cheese, onions in gravy ($1.75), chalupas de pollo (fried corn tortillas with chicken) for $1.50, fried pork Mexican style ($1.50), chulaqueles with eggs, sausage, beans and salad ($1.75), fried beans (75 cents), guacamole (75 cents), chile con carne (80 cents). Portions in every case were more than adequate and neatly arranged on the plate.

For a novel dessert the menu lists thick milk shakes of pineapple, mango, melon, banana and lemon. Espresso is very good and is only 15 cents, the same price as the American coffee.

Mi Tierra, in addition to its good food, provides an interesting experience. The critical question for the individual diner to decide for himself is whether his discomfort threshold is high enough to endure some of the environmental difficulties.

Telephone:	586-9278
Days Open:	7 days
Hours Open:	10 A.M. to midnight
Bar:	Yes
Air Conditioning:	Yes
Recommended for:	Lunch. Dinner. Dating.
Your Comments:	
Food:	Good
Ambiance:	Good
Hygiene:	Good
Service:	Good

Molfetas, 307 W. 47th Street, is a well-established Greek cafeteria and restaurant set in a quiet side street just within vaulting distance of the old Madison Square Garden. Molfetas is popular with a section of the sporting crowd, and on the evening of a big event Molfetas' atmosphere becomes charged with a robust liveliness. Molfetas is in the Greek "taverna" tradition, which means that the kitchen displays its culinary accomplishments like a living menu. The diner is invited to survey the available items and make his selection.

Molfetas, up a few steps from the street level, actually has two floors, but most of the action takes place on the street floor. The room itself, recently remodeled in the formica mode, is long, clean and generally comfortable. There are booths along both sides of the room and tables are distributed from front to rear along the center area. The kitchen is the focal point at the rear of the room, and if you prefer self-service, trays and silverware are nearby. The chefs behind the moisture-clouded protective glass over the steam table are helpful, pleasant men. Nick Triantafillou, a twinkling little man who has been with Molfetas for 12 years, is particularly open and gracious, as is his brother George. In any event, the chefs will describe their dishes good-naturedly and do not hesitate to lift cover after cover off the huge pots so that your eye as well as your palate can be stimulated. The display has a homey attraction, and making up one's mind is not always easy. You will find the countermen reasonably patient.

Some traditional starters are grape leaves (65 cents), taramosalata (caviar and soft cheese mixture) for 50 cents, cold stuffed tomatoes for 90 cents (authors' choice) and cold string beans. In Greek cooking lamb is the principal meat. Molfetas offers lamb with potato ($1.30), lamb oregano ($1.35), lamb with vegetables ($1.30), a good-sized piece of either shank or shoulder stewed with vegetables, an authors' choice, leg of lamb for $1.60 (a properly cooked pink lamb) (an authors' choice), shoulder of lamb ($1.60), lamb with spaghetti ($1.35), moussaka for $1.30—this is alternating layers of broad noodles and ground meat with a light puff paste topping, cooked in a tomato-based sauce, (authors' choice), pastitsio ($1.30), a macaroni and meat combination; spinach pie (90 cents). Fish is also on the menu, and the broiled porgy, bass ($1.40) and stewed codfish or calama ($1.40) are frequently served. All dishes come with a generous helping of two, and sometimes three, vegetables. Rice is the mainstay, and spinach, potatoes, spaghetti, eggplant or other stewed vegetables fill out the available complement. Portions are extremely liberal, and you will carry away a well-laden plate. Salad is a good counterpoint, and there is always a Greek salad (35 cents) or separate dishes of sliced tomatoes or black olives. Oil and vinegar dressing is provided from two separate bottles which the counterman shakes over the salad like a barber applying hair tonic.

For dessert there are the honey-soaked Greek pastries—baklava, galactoboureko (authors' choice), among others, at 35 cents; rice pudding (35 cents), yogurt or melon and other fruit in season provide the rest of the selections. A freshly made cup of Greek coffee is only 15 cents and is very good. Greek wine, which goes so well with the food, is 50 cents for a large glass of retsina (the Greeks' resinated wine, which generally requires an acquired taste) or roditys, a dry rose which is more to the average taste. Service is available from the short-jacketed, trim waiters, who are prompt and efficient.

The jukebox is furnished solely with Greek music and provides a lively background. Lunchtime is generally peaceful and not overly crowded. In the evening, when the crowd begins to fill the brightly lighted room and the sensuous Greek music combines with strong wine and good, solid food, the atmosphere becomes a bit heady, but there's no dancing in the aisles. That occurs on the upper floor, where there is entertainment and dancing every evening except Tuesday. The festivities have their effect on the price of the dishes.

:	WO 2-8650
:	7 days
en:	11 A.M. to 3 P.M
itioning:	No
ended for:	Lunch. Dating.
mments:	
	Excellent
ce:	Good
e:	Good
:	Good

Telephone:	624-9257
Days Open:	7 days
Hours Open:	11:30 A.M. to 8:30 P.M.
Bar:	No
Air Conditioning:	Yes
Recommended for:	Lunch. Dinner. Dating.
Your Comments:	
Food:	Good
Ambiance:	Fair to Good
Hygiene:	Excellent
Service:	Good

The Near East Restaurant, 138 Court Street, a Syrian restaurant is just a door away from Atlantic Avenue, the main street o Brooklyn Heights' substantial Arab community. The restaurant well established in the neighborhood, has a good-sized Aral clientele but is also popular with many of the other resident of the area. It is a small (seating 40), unpretentious restauran of one neatly painted (tan) room with a high and beautifu corrugated tin ceiling. A few chromo reproductions are hun about the room, but its most impressive visual quality is its ex traordinary cleanliness. When all the tables are neatly set wit their brilliant white napery, shining silverware and glasse flanked by plastic and chromium chairs, the appearance of th room is almost clinical. The menu is small, but it carries a basi complement of familiar Syrian dishes. The daily changes add on or another special dish. The stuffed lamb rib ($1.00), one dis not frequently encountered in Oriental restaurants, is a flaye lamb rib wrapped about a filling of rice, nuts and ground mea and steamed in its own broth (authors' choice). Mushrooms an meat is a healthy dish of large whole mushrooms and smal pieces of lamb cooked in an onion and butter broth for $1.2 (authors' choice). Some of the other Syrian dishes include bake kibee for $1.00 (described on page 25), rolled cabbage for $1.0 (a ground-meat, nut and rice mixture cooked in a rolled cabbag leaf), string beans and meat ($1.00), broiled lamb liver ($1.25) baked vegetables ($1.00), baba ganouge (90 cents). The ver familiar shish kebab is $2.00. A variety plate of assorted meat is $1.75. A separate accompanying dish of buttered rice is 2 cents. Some of the available dishes which make excellent starter are the hommus (70 cents), white cheese (feta) for 40 cents, o cucumbers in laban (a yogurt sauce) for 50 cents. A very larg fresh vegetable salad is 70 cents, but it can serve two. Dessert are limited to a milk pudding (25 cents), stewed apricots (4 cents) and a choice of halvah (35 cents) or Oriental pastry a 50 cents. The thick Turkish coffee (15 cents) is the perfec beverage to end a Syrian meal.

At the Near East, Mr. Shiner is the cook and Mrs. Shiner occasionally assisted by a waitress, takes care of the tables. The

small family staff make
lantic Avenue is the bes
interesting Saturday can
with a leisurely lunch or

Telephone:
Days Ope
Hours Op
Bar: N
Air Cond
Recomm
Your C
Food:
Ambia
Hygien
Servic

Nom Wah's, 13 Doyers Street, is the most venerable of the Chinese tea parlors. Dim-Sum is served continually every day from 11 to 3 by roving waitresses (not all of whom speak English) carrying amply laden trays. Dim-Sum is a somewhat ambiguous word; as a noun it is best translated as a dumpling, but when used to describe the luncheon, it takes on a considerably larger meaning. The Dim-Sum luncheon is, in point of fact, a spectacular array of small, almost snack-like, delicacies served with the appropriate tea. Though Dim-Sum is the generic term for the feast, it hardly describes the range of items which are served. The offering is large and impressive, and one may select dishes at will. At the conclusion of the meal the waitress determines the bill by counting the piles of small and large oval serving dishes, somewhat like a porcelain abacus. Small dishes represent 50 cents, and the large ones 70 cents. Some restaurants in Chinatown will serve a Dim-Sum tea luncheon only at noon on Sunday. There are other tea parlors scattered about the area, resembling very modest American luncheonettes. There, Dim-Sum is served at counters throughout the day. Their choice, however, is considerably less than Nom Wah's.

The accompanying chart of Dim-Sum varieties and ingredients is designed to take some of the bewilderment out of the tea luncheon and leave it as the wondrous, pleasurable experience it is. In any case, Nom Wah's gracious lady in charge, Madam May Choy, is on hand and will offer help if needed.

BOW YEE (Sheemy)—3 FOR 50¢

One of the class of closely packed chopped pork and Chinese vegetable mixtures not enclosed in a dough wrapper. They differ in their toppings. This has a slice of abalone.

TIM JUE SHEEMY—3 FOR 50¢

Same basic mixture as Bow Yee. Somewhat more colorful because of its green pepper base and red and white shredded lobster topping.

TOONG GUOO SHEEMY—3 FOR 50¢

The now familiar sheemy mixture crowned with a Chinese black mushroom.

HAK SHEEMY—3 FOR 50¢

This species is decorative. The sheemy mixture is embraced by flayed, flattened shrimp.

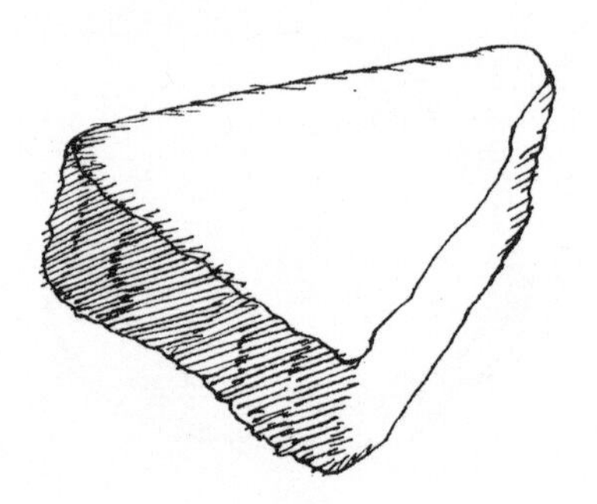

LOP CHEUNG—3 FOR 50¢

Again the chopped pork mixture, this time topped by a spicy Chinese sausage. Sheemy of this class are steamed for fifteen minutes.

DOW SHEW SHEEMY—3 FOR 50¢

A different type of sheemy made of bean curd stuffed with ground pike. The curd is light yellow with a firm custard-like texture. It is quite bland and may require getting used to.

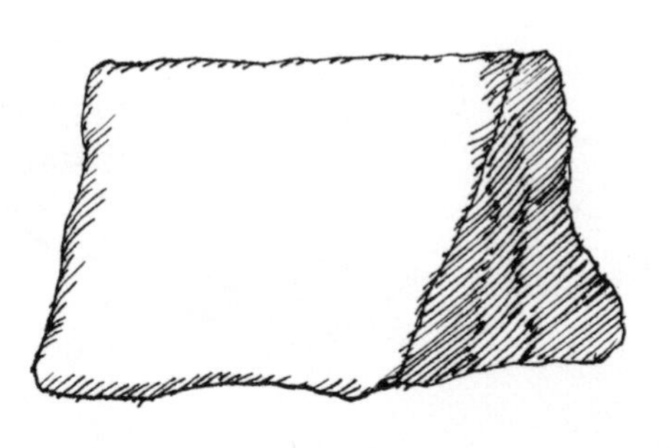

JOW—3 FOR 50¢

A wedge of fried bean curd. The frying technique produces a change in curd skin texture from the steamed variety, but the flavor remains elusive.

YEE YOOK LOT JUE SHEEMY—3 FOR 50¢

A ground pike fishball festooned with Chinese sausage at top and green pepper at bottom.

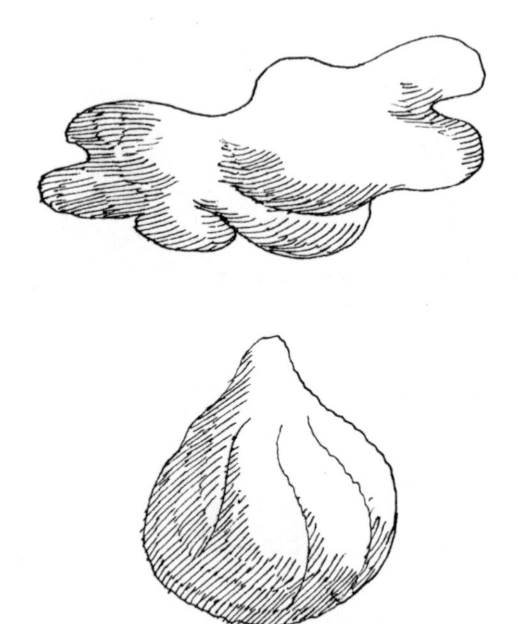

SUEY GOW—3 FOR 50¢

A shrimp and vegetable mixture wrapped in a wrinkled, yellow noodle-like covering. This steamed dish has a strong fish flavor which some may find too insistent.

HAR GOW—4 FOR 50¢

A delicate combination of tiny shrimp and water chestnuts encased in shiny white rice flour dough and steamed for five minutes.

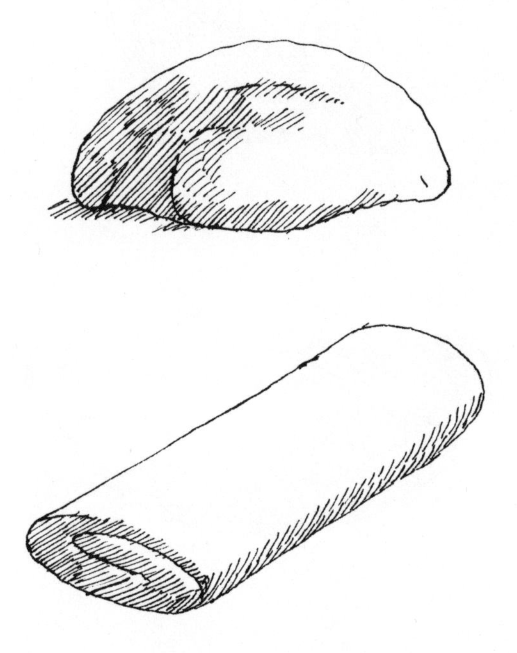

FUN GWOR—3 FOR 50¢

A steam cooked mixture of chopped crabmeat, peas and Chinese vegetables wrapped in white translucent rice flour dough.

FUN GOON—3 FOR 50¢

A shiny rice flour envelope roll filled with bean sprouts, water chestnuts, pork and mushrooms, steamed.

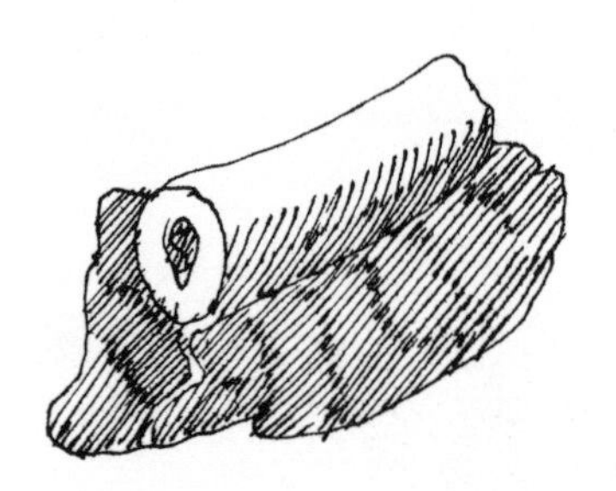

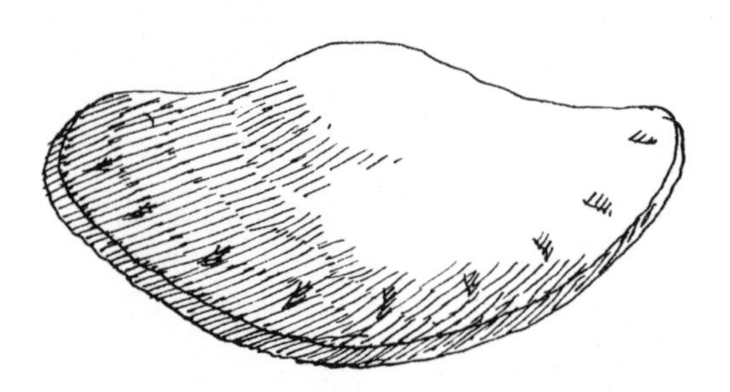

PIE GUAT—SMALL DISH—50¢

Inch-long sections of spareribs in a delicious brown mixture of Hoisin* and oyster sauces.

GAR LAY GORK—2 FOR 50¢

A curried pork turnover. The pastry dough covering is uncharacteristically thick. It is extremely tasty and somewhat Indian in flavor.

* Hoisin sauce, often used as a marinade base, is made from soy beans, sugar and food color.

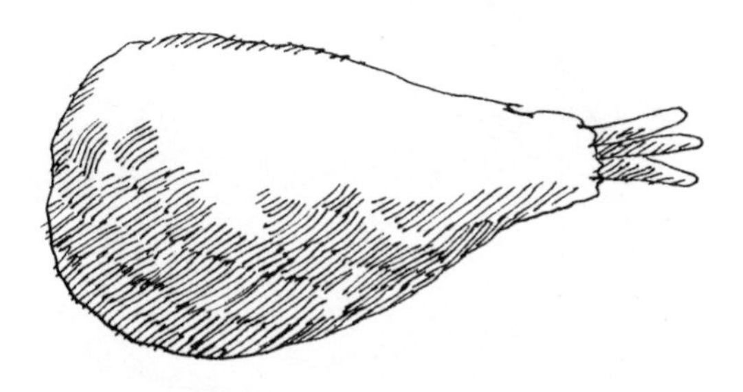

GAI GOON—2 FOR 70¢

Chopped chicken, bean sprouts, Chinese cabbage, water chestnuts and mushrooms, wrapped in an omelette, all dipped in batter, then deep fried. A popular favorite.

JAR HAR—4 FOR 70¢

This is simply shrimp dipped in a batter made of flour and water and then deep-fried. Through some inscrutable process, it comes to the table inflated to the size of a large chicken leg.

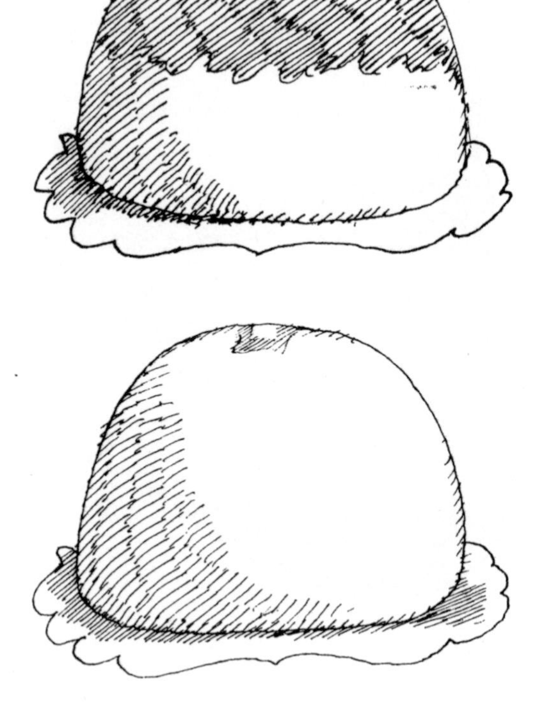

GOOK SHAR SHEW BOW—25¢ EACH

A large baked bun with a sweet roast pork filling. This is more like a bread than any of the other dumplings.

*JING SHAR SHEW BOW—15¢ DISH

The steamed version of the bow family. It has a simple, imposing purity about it. The filling is identical but its outer texture is softer and lighter than its baked brother.

* Bow and other pastries can be purchased for home consumption at Nom Wah's Bakery adjacent to the restaurant.

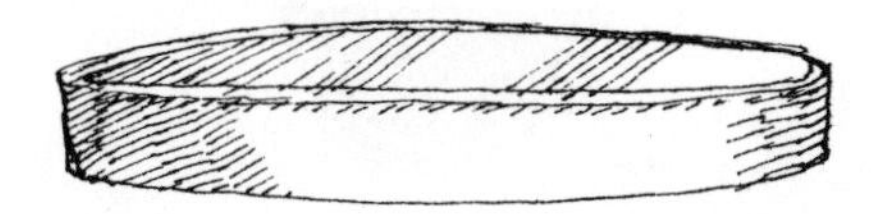

TEEM BOW—15¢ EACH

These are sweet dessert variations with soybean, peanut butter or lotus seed fillings.

DIM SUM—3 FOR 50¢

An open-top ground pork and Chinese vegetable combination, surrounded tightly by a won ton dough wrapper.

Telephone: EL 5-9141	
Days Open: 6 days (Closed Sunday)	
Hours Open: 11 A.M. to 6 P.M.	
Bar: Beer only	
Air Conditioning: Yes	
Recommended for: Lunch. Dating.	
Your Comments:	
Food: Good	
Ambiance: Good	
Hygiene: Good	
Service: Poor to Fair	

Nyborg & Nelson, 937 Second Avenue (between 49th and 50th streets), is a Scandinavian lunch parlor and delicatessen. The restaurant side of the combination came into being as a device to attract customers to the items available for sale in the food shop. In that attractive area one can find a wonderful array of Scandinavian delicacies. Tiny, fresh crayfish either live or boiled with dill are arranged alongside a dazzling range of yellow cheeses, pink smoked salmon, dark-brown Swedish bread loaves, gold-and-silver-foil-wrapped Norwegian and Danish beers, silvery Baltic herring, stacks of tinned fish and lavishly packaged biscuits and cookies. The refrigerated showcase, behind which sandwiches and smorgasbord plates are prepared, offers its own glistening selection of cold meats and salads. Sandwiches are the main support of the lunchroom menu, and the ingredients of each item listed are clearly visible in the glass-faced refrigerator.

The exceptions are the one hot-plate daily special and the occasional soup. The soups are truly extraordinary, and if you are fortunate enough to find the yellow pea or asparagus soups on any particular day, you'll find either one a rare treat. The hot dishes are Scandinavian: beef à la Lindstrom, two meat patties erved with sweet brown beans and lingonberries; meat-filled potato dumplings; Thursdays only, Swedish pancakes with lingonberries are served; and on Fridays, fried fileted Baltic herring. The prices of the daily specials range from $1.50 to $1.75. A racefully arranged smorgasbord plate—small, $1.50, large $2.00 —is a nice way to sample a variety of salads, fish and cold meats. Two slices of excellent whole grained dark bread and the ghter anise-flavored limpa or crisp Swedish crackers accompany the main dish. Highlights from the sandwich list include smoked eel ($1.10), rolled beef with pickled beets ($1.00), Westphalian ham ($1.10), liver paté with cucumber (95 cents), egg and anchovies (90 cents) and veal loaf with pickled beets (90 cents). Cucumber, beet-and-apple and potato salads (25 cents) are available as a small side order. There is a small and changing selection of delicate, tasty cookies (25 cents to 35 cents). Coffee is very good (20 cents). The best of domestic and imported beers (40 cents to 70 cents) are also available. The orwegian Rignes (50 cents) is a pleasant light beer accompaniment to a sandwich luncheon. Portions are on the small side, and in terms of quantity alone Nyborg & Nelson is not good value by *Underground Gourmet* standards. Two dollars spent here will leave the robust eater hungry. Nyborg & Nelson's redeeming features are superb freshness and attractive presentations of its food and its unusual menu. Though the waitresses are pleasant and attentive, the service, for some reason, remains erratic.

Telephone: TR 9-1199
Days Open: 7 days
Hours Open: 11 A.M. to 11 P.M.
Bar: Yes
Air Conditioning: Yes
Recommended for: Lunch. Dating.
Your Comments:
Food: Good to Excellent
Ambiance: Good
Hygiene: Good
Service: Fair to Good

Oscar's (Salt of the Sea), 1155 Third Avenue (between 67th and 68th streets), serves seafood at prices somewhat lower than the general run of good seafood restaurants but still a cut above the *Underground Gourmet* price level. What principally qualifies Oscar's for inclusion in this book are the daily luncheon specials. These consist of Manhattan or New England chowder, a fish of the day with rice or French-fried potatoes and cole slaw, dessert and beverage. Both chowders are splendid. The New England is white, creamy smooth and loaded with tender clams; the Manhattan, a somewhat thinner broth, is red, spicy, invigorating and also filled with clams. Simple economics dictate that the fish of the day be chosen from the more plentiful and less expensive varieties available on the market. Fortunately, many excellent fish may be found within these limitations. A sample choice can include broiled Boston mackerel, broiled porgie or broiled flounder. The price of the complete luncheon is $1.69 for the mackerel or $1.99 for flounder or porgie. The fish is fresh, never overcooked and the portions are generous. The accompanying cole slaw could well serve as a model for how this usually banal dish can be made palatable. Dessert is either gelatin or rice pudding. The coffee is first-rate. There are a few dishes on the à la carte menu where the selective diner can eat in the neighborhood of $2.00. There is filet of flounder, scrod or fried smelts each at $1.95; whole flounder and fish and chips are $1.85. Oscar's stews, made with half cream, half milk and sherry are quite special and inexpensive. The three choices—clam, oyster and scallop—are only $1.50 each. The light eater may find the steamed soft-shell clams or mussels with garlic broth at $1.75 or the baked cherrystone clams with bacon and cheese ($1.50) enough for a filling meal. Oscar's generosity extends to the table bread basket, which is filled with sea toast, salt sticks and onion rolls.

In general, the service is efficient, but because of the crowds at peak hours, it may slow up. Oscar—he is the one in the black shirt and trousers—has developed this restaurant from a small eating place under the Third Avenue El into a bustling institution by offering good, fresh fish, healthy portions and fair prices.

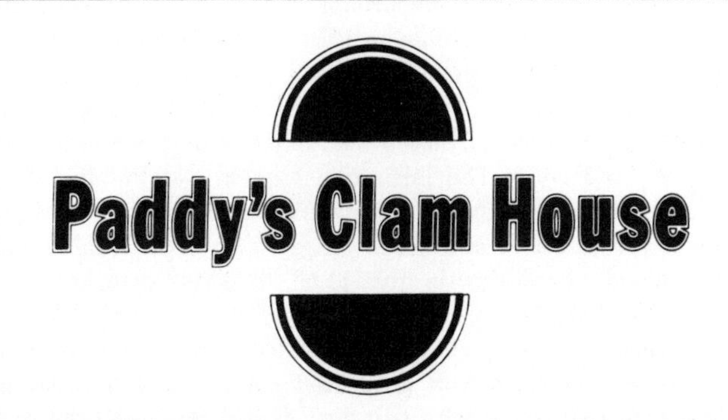

Telephone:	244-9123
Days Open:	7 days
Hours Open:	M. through Sat., 10:30 A.M. to 9:45 P.M.; Sun., 11:30 A.M. to 9 P.M.
Bar:	Beer only
Air Conditioning:	Yes
Recommended for:	Lunch. Dinner. Dating.
Your Comments:	
Food:	Good
Ambiance:	Excellent
Hygiene:	Good
Service:	Good to Excellent

This 60-year-old seafood emporium, 215 W. 34th Street, has managed to maintain an authentic 1930 seaside-resort atmosphere in the midst of the Macy–Gimbel–34th Street complex. It is a long, simply furnished restaurant. Tables, counters and partition-like walls are painted in the clearly dated color combination of pale green and ivory. The institutional quality of Paddy's does not detract from the quality, preparation and enjoyment of its extensive menu. There is a broad range of broiled, steamed and fried seafood specialties in the $1.60 to $2.00 category, but Paddy's big bargains are the lunch and dinner specials. The authors sampled the lunch which included a white Boston-style fish chowder crammed with good-sized chunks of fish followed by broiled scrod served with two tasty boiled potatoes; the dessert was a liberal portion of nesselrode pie and a cup of above-average coffee, all for $1.48. A different fish is available each day as the luncheon special, and one may choose from an assortment of appetizers and desserts. The dinner, with larger portions, is about $1.00 more but still represents excellent value. An unusual dish from the à la carte menu is freshly shucked fried mussels ($1.75).

The staff of Paddy's seems to have come with the period decor. The waiters and waitresses are mostly middle-aged, long-time employees who have retained a professional concern for the patron. Their service is prompt, and despite the hubbub (Paddy's serves about 3,000 daily) they are seldom abrupt. The interesting items are steamed soft clams, hot broth and butter ($1.00); rainbow brook trout ($1.80); steamed finnan haddie ($1.85). There is no bar, but a choice of domestic and imported beer is available at popular prices.

Telephone:	LO 3-2581
Days Open:	7 days
Hours Open:	11 A.M. to 1 A.M.
Bar:	Yes
Air Conditioning:	Yes
Recommended for:	Lunch. Dinner. Dating.
Your Comments:	
Food:	Fair to Good
Ambiance:	Good
Hygiene:	Fair to Good
Service:	Fair to Good

Paradise Oriental Restaurant, 311 W. 41st Street, across the street from the Port Authority Bus Terminal, is one of the largest Greek restaurants of the Greek enclave in the West 40s. The room is very large and high-ceilinged, and with its formidable bar in the front and busy serving station in the rear there is a cafeterialike quality about the place. Service is carried out by very active, red-jacketed young Greek waiters who in the main are quite good-looking and courteous. The lively, vigorous feeling of this uptown emporium comes from its youthful clientele, principally college students and Greeks of all ages.

The food, consistent with the atmosphere, has a robust peasantlike character. There is nothing elegant about the Paradise Inn. The dishes are tasty and the portions are generous. For habitués of Greek restaurants the menu offers little or no surprise; however, the range of dishes is large and varied. The traditional openers are either taramosalata at 55 cents (a smooth, pale-pink mixture of red caviar, oil and bread paste) and avgolemono soup (25 cents), a thick pale-yellow mixture of egg, lemon and rice. Both are flavorful. Other first courses include salads and a variety of Greek cheeses: feta (30 cents), casseri (35 cents), kefaloteri (35 cents), and saganabi (in casserole) at 65 cents. Tripe soup at 50 cents (one author's obsession) is particularly good. It consists of well-cooked tripe in the aforementioned rich avgolemono soup. The entrée menu is distributed among an ample selection of lamb, chicken and fish dishes. Particularly noteworthy in the lamb section is kapama à la Paradise ($1.25), a lamb shank stewed with vegetables and Oriental meatballs for $1.00 (an authors' choice), which is made of ground lamb flavorfully spiced with rosemary and served in the ubiquitous avgolemono sauce. For those favorably disposed toward lamb there is either leg, loin or shoulder to choose from at $1.50 each. Other good dishes are chicken casserole ($1.10) and fried squid ($1.25). Two fine dishes are the spinach and cheese pie for 75 cents (alternate layers of cheese and spinach within a flaky thin crust) (authors' choice) and artichokes à la polita for 75 cents (stewed artichokes in a white viscous sauce). Desserts emphasize a full line of Greek pastry (35 cents); in addition there is yogurt (25 cents), rice pudding (25 cents), or fresh fruit of the season (35 cents). Greek coffee (picro—no sugar; metrio—medium sweet, Glico Cafe—sweet) is only 15 cents. The bar prices are particularly reasonable, and the ouzo (Greek anise) at 65 cents is probably the cheapest in the city. The Paradise, under the leadership of John Petrisas, has grown from the small quarters it once occupied on the same street, but despite its largeness it has retained a friendly and intimate spirit. It is an especially good place to go to with a large party.

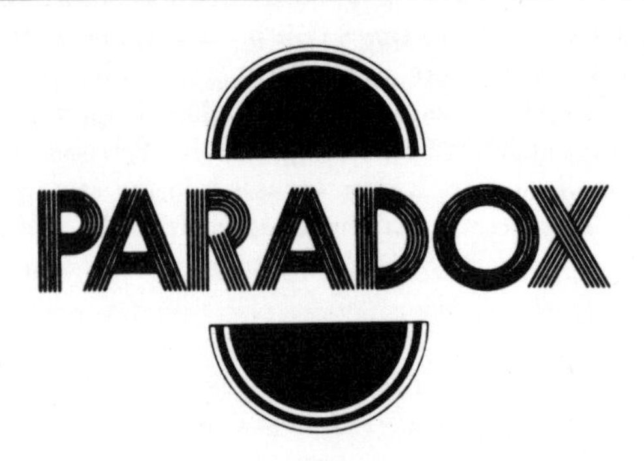

Telephone: GR 3-9168

Days Open: 7 days

Hours Open: 5:30 P.M. to 11:30 P.M.

Bar: No

Air Conditioning: Yes

Recommended for: Dinner. Dating?

Your Comments:

Food: Fair to Good

Ambiance: Good

Hygiene: Poor

Service: Good

Paradox, 64 E. 7th Street, may be New York's hippest restaurant. It is a focal point and meeting place for Zen Buddhists, League for Spiritual Discovery followers, McLuhanites, vegetarians, partisans of the New Left, artists, art students, poets and any or all of East Village cultists. The restaurant is a below-street-level large room that seats about 75 to 100 persons, depending on how the tables are arranged. Through the center of the room is a row of tables joined together to make one continuous communal eating surface. One sits wherever there is a free chair. You take pot luck with your eating companion, but more often than not he will be interesting and even friendly. For those who want more privacy there is a random assortment of tables seating two to four each along the side walls. The room is lit by brown-paper-bag shaded lamps which hang above the center row of tables. Public notices and posters are the only other decorative touches. The range of subjects includes macrobiotic food sources, off-Broadway shows, human be-ins (a friendly gathering), yoga lessons, poetry readings, protest meetings, apartments and roommates wanted, new titles at East Village bookshops and assorted calls to action. The inscriptions on the lavatory walls are by far the most literate in New York.

The kitchen is at the rear of the dining area where one orders from the large posted menu. After ordering, you find a seat and the pleasant waitress who took your order somehow manages to find you in the usually crowded room. After you've finished with the meal you return to the rear and the same waitress will take your money pleasantly. The food is prepared according to macrobiotic dietary principles. These include the use of organically grown (no commercial fertilizers or pesticides) vegetables, a balance of yin and yang (too complicated to explain here), and the exclusion of many foods considered injurious to good health, such as meats, refined sugar and various dairy products. Unrefined rice and grains, vegetables and fish are the principal ingredients of the dishes offered by the Paradox. The most popular dish is the shrimp and rice platter, which consists of a large helping of brown rice with a red bean or vegetable gravy, a chunk of squash, a mound of pickled seaweed, a helping of raw cabbage salad and about seven plump fresh-cooked shrimp (authors' choice) for $1.90. The taste of this dish is both bland and tasty, and it is filling. The same platter is available with either swordfish, butterfish or bass in place of the shrimps at the same price. By choosing mackerel or sole the price is reduced to $1.65. The menu changes slightly, according to what is available at the market, but it is always quite limited. The aforementioned dishes represent the heart of it. Lesser dishes are very good, especially the vegetable soup at 45 cents (authors' choice). Available also are a bowl of rice (25 cents), with dressing (45 cents), and bread (35 cents), a special preparation of whole grain flours, which accounts for its high price. For dessert there is Indian rice and semolina pudding at 45 cents each. The latter was a glutinous drag. Coffee is high on the forbidden list, but the tea is free, which you pour yourself from a steaming pot that rests on an electric plate along the left brick wall. Sesame seed is served at the table as a salt substitute. Chopsticks are there, too, as well as a fork if you prefer.

The atmosphere of the Paradox is truly unusual. There is a strong sense of community about the restaurant that may put a newcomer off for the first time. The food is good, if limited, but eating at the Paradox is an out-of-the-ordinary gastrodelic happening.

Telephone:	MU 4-9625
Days Open:	7 days
Hours Open:	11 A.M. to 11 P.M.
Bar:	Yes
Air Conditioning:	Yes
Recommended for:	Lunch. Dating.
Your Comments:	
Food:	Fair to Good
Ambiance:	Fair
Hygiene:	Fair
Service:	Fair to Good

The Philippine Garden, 455 Second Avenue (at 26th Street), is one of the few Philippine restaurants in the city. Considering the long association of the Philippines with the United States, it seems odd that there are not more. The food is quite palatable and acceptable to the American taste.

Physically, the Philippine Garden is divided into two dimly lit rooms each seating 35 people. The pseudo-tropical decor of a bamboo lattice festooned with an assortment of plastic jungle flora is less offensive than one might expect. This restaurant is another of those whose à la carte dinner menu soars well beyond our price level, but the seven-course luncheon offers a sensational bargain. Luncheon ranges from a low of $1.00 to a high of $1.35, and it includes soup, egg roll, mixed vegetables, rice, a main course, dessert and beverage. The authors suggest commencing with a shrimp soup, which is a thin, pale Japaneselike broth punctuated on the surface by a sprinkling of floating greens and tiny pink shrimps lining the bottom of the bowl. From the 14 entrées available we recommend the adobo ($1.35), a spicy, highly garlicked mixture of vinegar-marinated chicken and pork, and stuffed shrimps at $1.35—one of those inscrutable culinary feats which inflate shrimps to huge proportions. In the stuffed-items category there are chicken and crab, also at $1.35. Spare-ribs ($1.35) are done in the Chinese manner, with a strong sweet-and-sour sauce. Other interesting dishes include a Philippine meat roll ($1.35) and eshabetoe ($1.25), fried fish with a sweet-and-sour sauce. At the bottom of the price scale are three fish dishes: squid, fried fish and grilled fish ($1.10).

The egg roll clearly shows its Chinese influence, and the mixed vegetables are a sauté of difficult-to-identify greens. Both dishes make a tasty accompaniment to the main course. Meats at the Philippine Garden appear of indifferent quality, but the spices and marinades which are characteristic of the Philippine cooking style overcome any tastelessness.

There are three desserts, but the best is the baked banana (a ripe yellow banana baked in a thin translucent crust of coconut oil and sugar), a very good dish indeed. Coffee is good enough but the ginger tea offers an authentic and aromatic end to a fine meal.

Telephone:	233-9523
Days Open:	7 days
Hours Open:	11 A.M. to 10 P.M.
Bar:	No
Air Conditioning:	Yes
Recommended for:	Lunch. Dinner. Dating.
Your Comments:	
Food:	Good to Excellent
Ambiance:	Fair
Hygiene:	Fair
Service:	Good

Ping Chin, 81 Mulberry Street, is the archetype of the small Chinese restaurant—a small bare room, formica tables, 24 seats, all seasonings on the table, the cook-owner working in the kitchen and one waiter. At Ping Chin the cook is visible from the dining room, and watching his quiet, graceful competence you can genuinely anticipate that the food is going to be well prepared, which indeed it is. It seems to us that these anonymous cooks in the small Chinatown restaurants have appreciably greater skill and range than their counterparts in the other ethnic sections of the city.

The nature of Chinese cooking permits a small restaurant like Ping Chin to offer a menu of about 100 dishes. The pressures of popular taste have forced the owner to list a short accommodating list of Cantonese dishes, but the heart of the menu is Mandarin style. This enables the diner to enjoy a spicy, aromatic soup such as pickle and sliced pork at $1.20 large, 80 cents medium, 50 cents small (authors' choice), and a medium-sized portion will serve three nicely. Other excellent soups include mushroom and sliced chicken, mushroom and bean cake, ham and vegetable, hot and sour, all priced the same as the pickle and pork.

The dumpling assortment is larger than the usual Chinese restaurant offering. For a description of the basic dumpling, see page 126. These come in three preparations: boiled, ten for $1.00; fried and steamed, ten for $1.20. The special tien tsui pastry (five for $1.00) is a white, soft, chewy dough bun about the size of a breakfast roll and filled with ground pork, Chinese vegetables and spices. An order of these buns would make an ample though somewhat one-dimensional meal. A good side dish under the dumpling heading is a thick, rather heavy pancake with green onion (scallion) at 50 cents. Very thin pancakes at 10 cents each are available and they make excellent wrappings for some of the main courses. Fried rice comes in eight variations, prices ranging from 80 cents to $1.20. There are 15 variations of noodles, some cold, some fried, some in soup and some served hot with meat and/or sauce. Pasta lovers will particularly enjoy the char jang mein with azountice meat sauce (a white soft noodle with a lively brown sauce) for 85 cents. Though cold noodles sound unappetizing, they are in fact a refreshing kind of salad. One beautiful example is the dish called sesame sauce ($1.00), prepared with cold noodles, slivers of cucumbers, bean sprouts and a spoonful of a thick mixture of bean cake, sesame oil and soy sauce (authors' choice). Other choice dishes from the beef, pork, chicken, duck and seafood listings include chicken with hot green pepper ($1.50), sliced beef with bean preserve at $1.60 (authors' choice), sliced pork with bean sprouts covered with an omelet ($1.80), sweet-and-sour bok choy ($1.00), sautéed shrimp and kidney ($1.80), pot roast (woo shang) with Oriental spices ($1.00 small, $2.00 large).

Portions are quite generous, and a lone diner can be fed well on any one main dish. The hot peppery tea is served by the glassful and is replenished as desired. Many small Chinatown restaurants adhere to this style of tea service. Desserts are not listed.

Nothing can be said about the Ping Chin decor, for its only decoration is a large blue noisy air conditioner. The service is homey, and our young waiter was very friendly. Ping Chin offers nothing but good food.

Telephone: 226-8912

Days Open: 6 days (Closed Sunday)

Hours Open: 10 A.M. to 1 A.M.

Bar: No

Air Conditioning: No

Recommended for: Lunch. Dinner. Dating.

Your Comments:

Food: Fair to Good

Ambiance: Good

Hygiene: Fair

Service: Fair to Good

The Puglia Restaurant, 189 Hester Street, CA 6-8912, in Manhattan's Little Italy, is an authentic transplant of a southern Italian trattoria. Southern Italian cooking is in many ways a cuisine of poverty; it lacks the rich combination of butter, expensive cuts of meat, delicate vegetables and elaborate sauces that characterize the fare of central and northern Italy. It depends heavily on olive oil, garlic, spicy pizzaiuola sauce and whatever meats and vegetables are available and above all inexpensive. The Puglia is proud of its specialties—marricelli, mogliatelle, and cappozelle, which turn out to be in respective order sheep's intestines ($1.00), sheep's testicles (five for 75 cents) and sheep's head (50 cents for half a head). All are prepared over coals in the southern Italian manner. Other organ-meat specialties include soffrito (lung in sauce) at 75 cents; fried heart ($1.00); liver alla Genovese (fried with onions) at $1.00; and an excellent tripe (75 cents) in a semihot, pale orange sauce (an authors' choice). Other poor-people dishes that turn out to be first rate are macaroni and lentils, macaroni and ceci (chick-peas), macaroni and peas, all 75 cents each. The comic expression "pasta fazool," a corruption of pasta e fagiole, refers to these dishes. A delicious country dish also frequently available is verdura e ceci (75 cents), escarole and chick-peas cooked in a thick broth (an authors' choice). Other vegetable preparations include escarole sautéed in oil (75 cents), string-bean salad (75 cents), mushroom marinara (80 cents), onion salad (75 cents), broccoli rape (a bitter green), 75 cents plain and an inexplicable $1.00 when prepared with garlic. The range of pasta dishes—spaghetti, ziti percitelli, linguine, ravioli—all cooked to order, come with a broad spectrum of sauces: meatball, $1.25; sausage, $1.50; tomato, 75 cents; meat, $1.00; mushroom, $1.00 and marinara 75 cents. Other sauces include filet of anchovies prepared with olive oil and fried garlic (an authors' choice), 75 cents; garlic and oil, 75 cents; and clams, $1.10. More elaborate farinaceous dishes are ziti Siciliana made with egg plant, $1.25; lasagna, $1.25; and manicotti, $1.00. A little higher on the economic ladder there is a variety of veal dishes, scaloppine, cutlets, etc., ranging in price from $1.50 to $1.75. Portions are solid; service is informal and friendly. The espresso or demitasse is especially good and only 15 cents.

The restaurant's appearance has improved recently as the result of a paint job, but it is still far from a Forum of the Twelve Caesars. It is nonetheless roomy and comfortable, or, as the Puglia claims on its menu, "Un Vero Ritrovo Familare"—a friendly spot. The decorations include chromos of Pope Paul, Presidents Kennedy and Johnson and two signs reading "No singing or Dancing Allowed on Premises." This injunction is violated every Sunday when neighborhood families turn out en masse for dinner.

Telephone:	GR 7-7180
Days Open:	7 days
Hours Open:	11 A.M. to midnight
Bar:	Yes
Air Conditioning:	Yes
Recommended for:	Lunch. Dinner. Dating.
Your Comments:	
Food:	Good
Ambiance:	Fair
Hygiene:	Good
Service:	Fair to Good

Ralph's is a small family-run pizzeria cum restaurant located at 347 First Avenue, (20th Street) in the shadow of Peter Cooper Village. The owner, Ralph Ferrante, formerly a production foreman with La Rosa for nine years, knows how to cook spaghetti sensitively and serves it well and with a variety of sauces. One dish that had special appeal for the authors was a hard-to-find combination of spaghetti with garlic, oil and anchovies for $1.05. The antipasto at $1.75 is especially good. By adding a few original touches, such as stuffed breaded eggplant, to a liberal assortment of vegetables, meats and cheese, Ralph has converted the usual antipasto into a lusty offering. The portion is quite large and could easily serve as a meal for one or an ample first course for two. Meat, seafood and omelet dishes fill out the menu, but they lack the distinction of the pasta. An experimental type, Ralph has developed a competitively priced pizza of which he is especially proud. He modestly claims it is the best in the city and it may be. At any rate it is quite tasty and filling. One of the pleasant accompanying features of the meal is the relatively low price of the imported and domestic wines. Ralph's has a house wine of good quality at 35 cents a glass, and if you are feeling particularly affluent a quart of Negri Soave at $3.00 is an exceptional buy for two people or more.

By decorating his restaurant with an arbor of plastic grapes, flowers and a variety of colored electric lights, Ralph has attempted to evoke some spirit of his native Italy. He has not been entirely successful.

There is a small counter and a number of booths in the forward part of the restaurant. There is also a rear room and a small garden, both with tables.

Mrs. Ferrante and her young daughter do most of the serving, and they are courteous and pleasant. Ralph is on hand occasionally when he is not in the kitchen, and he will ask about your well-being in his straightforward, friendly manner.

Some typical entrées: Macaroni Sicilian style (with eggplant) ($1.25), Spaghetti with red or white clam sauce ($1.50), Neapolitan-style meat balls ($1.50), Mozzarella omelet ($.85).

Telephone:	CI 5-2580
Days Open:	7 days
Hours Open:	Noon to 1 A.M.
Bar:	Beer and wine
Air Conditioning:	Yes
Recommended for:	Lunch. Dinner. Dating.
Your Comments:	
Food:	Fair to Good
Ambiance:	Fair to Good
Hygiene:	Good
Service:	Fair to Good

Un Rincon Argentino (an Argentine corner), 1626 Broadway, is
actually in the middle of the block in the heart of the Times
Square area. There are two grills visible through the large street
window. All the meats are broiled there on charcoal fires. Broiled
meats, an Argentine specialty, are the mainstay of this restaurant
The Rincon has two dimly lit floors, wagon-wheel lighting fixtures
and vinyl ponyskin upholstery. There is a large mural downstairs
which depicts a scene in Buenos Aires looking very much like
Times Square.

The basic menu applies to dinner and luncheon and offers five
dishes within the *Underground Gourmet* price range. In addition
your place mat for the luncheon informs you that there are five
dishes for 99¢ each. They are (by number):

1. Soup and pork sausage sandwich, coffee or tea. 2. Milanesa (a thin breaded beef cutlet) with salad, bread and butter. 3 Pork sausage and gaucho pie (known also as empanada), finely ground spicy meat-filled pastry crescent. 4. Half chicken (broiled), salad, bread and butter. 5. Broiled shor ribs, salad, bread and butter.

The special luncheon is served until 4 P.M. but not on Saturdays
Sundays and holidays.

The regular menus offer many of the same dishes but a con
siderably larger portion. The milanesa, with a big helping o
French-fried potatoes, is $1.95. The combination plate of shor
ribs, sausage and gaucho pie for $1.95 (an authors' choice) i
a lot of meat for the money. The restaurant will give you hal
a chicken, pork sausage and gaucho pie for the same price
Broiled kidneys with French-fried potatoes or a churrasc
(broiled skirt steak), with the same accompaniment, are $1.9
each. The Rincon chefs have a knowing hand with beef, an
their meat dishes take on a robust, flavorful quality. A pleasar
small salad of tomatoes, lettuce and onions with an Argentir
dressing of oil, vinegar and herbs is 30 cents. Most of the twelv
desserts are of one or another variety of pudding and cost eithe
35 or 50 cents. The home-made bread pudding is excellent. Coffe
is very good. Service by waiters in gaucho attire is pleasant. Ju
be certain to give your order clearly.

The authors' idea of an excellent picnic dinner is to buy a foil-lined bag of five hot gaucho pies, 30 cents each, and eat them while watching a movie in one of the nearby theaters. Slightly perverse but delicious.

Telephone: 989-9442	
Days Open: 6 days (Closed Monday)	
Hours Open: Noon to 11 P.M.	
Bar: Yes	
Air Conditioning: Yes	
Recommended for: Lunch. Dinner. Dating.	
Your Comments:	
Food: Good	
Ambiance: Good	
Hygiene: Good	
Service: Good	

osetta's, 502 Sixth Avenue (at 13th Street), is in that part of
reenwich Village where living is quite conventional. In keeping
ith the area, this comfortable restaurant emphasizes the tradi-
onal values of restaurant operation. Rosetta's offers a large
enu of familiar and well-prepared dishes at reasonable prices
erved in attractive quarters. A small group of tables is arranged
ward the large street window. The main body of the restaurant
ontains the greater number of tables, all neatly set with red-and-
hite tablecloths. The arrangement and pleasant lighting makes
r an inviting scene.

The à la carte dinner and luncheon menus offer substantially
e same dishes, but the luncheon prices run from 30 to 50 cents
ss for most of the entrées. The pasta list is varied and offers a
umber of dishes not often found in inexpensive restaurants, such
s home-made green noodles alla Bolognese (broad, tasty noodles
ith a light meat sauce) for $1.75 at both lunch and dinner (au-
ors' choice); home-made noodles al Filetto with prosciutto
$1.75, lunch), a broad flat noodle in a robust tomato sauce with
nall pieces of prosciutto; spaghetti with mushroom sauce ($1.45,
nch; $1.75, dinner). Rigatoni alla Rosetta ($2.00, lunch and
inner) and a redolent linguine aglio and olio with anchovies
$1.45, lunch; $1.75, dinner) are two basic southern Italian
shes. Also included under the pasta heading are a light meat
violi ($1.45, lunch; $1.75, dinner) and a tasty manicotti ($1.45,
nch; $1.75, dinner). The pasta is made at the restaurant and is
vorful and considerably superior to the average Italian res-
urant. It is cooked to order. The menu is quite extensive and
ere is no lack of choice among the meat, seafood and other
adings. Some selections of interest include veal scaloppine
mon sauce ($1.85, lunch), rather large, thin slices of tender
al delicately sautéed in a piquant lemon oil and butter sauce
uthors' choice); veal cutlet Milanese ($1.85, lunch), a breaded
in slice of veal; mussels arreganata ($1.55, lunch), mussels
ked on the half shell with bread crumbs, oil, garlic, parsley
d oregano; veal scaloppine al prosciutto ($1.95, lunch), thin
ices of veal sautéed in oil and butter with prosciutto covering;
d mushrooms à la Italiana ($1.50, lunch), sautéed with garlic,
and parsley.

All the dishes come with a vegetable, generally an oil-and
garlic flavored cooked spinach and a light potato croquette. Por
tions of the entrées are not large, but they are adequate. Th
desserts and salads are somewhat expensive, but if the price o
your entrée permits, the Italian cheese cake at 55 cents is par
ticularly good and, needless to say, calorific.

Rosetta's appetizers and soup prices are the same for luncheo
and dinner. A pleasant beginning to the meal can be had fro
either the spinach or escarole in broth for 50 cents (authors
choice).

Rosetta's presents a better than average Neapolitan bill of far
in an agreeable atmosphere. The number of dishes available a
prices within the *Underground Gourmet* range enables the dine
to select an excellent meal without too much trouble. The sta
is adequate and the service is professionally competent.

Telephone:	565-6161
Days Open:	7 days (Closed July and August)
Hours Open:	M. through F., 11:30 A.M. to 3 P.M., 5 P.M. to 10 P.M.; Sat., Sun., 1 P.M. to 8 P.M.
Bar:	Beer and wine
Air Conditioning:	Yes
Recommended for:	Lunch. Dinner. Dating.
Your Comments:	
Food:	Good
Ambiance:	Fair to Good
Hygiene:	Good
Service:	Good

The San Remo, 393 Eighth Avenue (between 29th and 30th streets), is a small luncheonette-restaurant surrounded by belly dance *palaces* and Greek eateries. The San Remo has a displaced gondola on its yellow plastic sign, but, accuracy of symbols and menu spelling aside, its food is quite commendable.

There is a conventional luncheonette counter that seats 14, several white plastic booths and assorted tables that seat about another 35. The room is neat, clean and ordinary, and the decor leans heavily on stainless steel and formica. In this undistinguished setting, the dishes and their preparation come as a pleasant surprise. Prosciutto and melon (rarely found in inexpensive Italian restaurants) is an excellent value at 45 cents (lunch) and 65 cents (dinner). The stracciatella (beaten egg and spinach in chicken broth) is 35 cents at lunch and 50 cents at dinner. The big surprises come in the delicate preparation of some of the main dishes. Scaloppine a la Genovese (authors' choice), $1.65 at dinner, is a tender thin veal slice lightly coated with egg batter and saturated with butter. It is served with spaghetti. The tomato sauce deserves special commendation because it is well balanced, properly cooked and made with *good* olive oil and fresh tomatoes. It stands in marked contrast to the viscous overcooked red paste served in most restaurants of this price range. Pollo alla valdostana ($1.40 at lunch, $1.65 at dinner), an authors' choice, is boned breast of chicken enclosing prosciutto and cheese, served with black mushrooms floating in a buttery sauce. Bravo! The good-looking lasagna ($1.10 at lunch, $1.35 at dinner) tastes as good as it looks. Other worthwhile finds are fettucine ($1.30, dinner only), another rarity for an inexpensive restaurant; sausage and peppers ($1.35); calf's liver with onions, butter and sauce ($1.35 at dinner); cheese mushroom and pepper omelet ($1.05); scaloppine a la Marsala ($1.35 at lunch, $1.65 at dinner). As befits a restaurant in this area, there is a plebeian side to the menu. Hot hero sandwiches include veal parmigiana (75 cents), veal and peppers (70 cents), meatballs (65 cents), sausage and peppers (75 cents at lunch, 85 cents at dinner), eggplant parmigiana (85 cents). All main dishes are served with spaghetti, potatoes, a vegetable or a modest salad.

The dessert list is distinguished by three good imported cheeses: Bel Paese, Gorgonzola, Provolone, all at 50 cents. The sweet and beverage list is standard, with espresso coffee for 20 cents. Service is friendly and attentive.

Telephone:	675-1820
Days Open:	7 days
Hours Open:	11 A.M. to 10 P.M.
Bar:	No
Air Conditioning:	Yes
Recommended for:	Lunch. Dinner.
Your Comments:	
Food:	Good to Excellent
Ambiance:	Fair to Poor
Hygiene:	Fair
Service:	Good

Segunda Perla, 107 Clinton Street, is a tidy and well-stocked stand in the ethnically mixed Lower East Side. It serves a variety of cuchifritos. Although it still has a long way to go before it can replace the egg cream or the hero in the gustatory esteem of New York snackers, the cuchifrito is a fast-rising challenger. All over the city, particularly in the less posh areas, one can scarcely walk a block without encountering small open luncheonettes with signs, sometimes naïvely lettered, but always colorful, bearing the word "cuchifritos." The word, subject to some etymological debate, is generally conceded to mean "fried pork things." Indeed many of the arcane items that fill the windows of the open stands originate with and from the pig, but not all, to be sure. The authors, who would like to believe that their palates are relatively catholic, found cuchifritos an exotic and occasionally unnerving experience. For the intrepid eater we recommend an excursion to one of these home-style Puerto Rican food stands. The countermen, though accustomed to the neighborhood Puerto Rican trade, treat outsiders with a gentle encouragement and courteous interest.

EASY

PAPA RELLENA—15¢

Orange colored* dumpling like mashed potato mound, gently spiced with a ground pork filling—a Latin cousin to the knish.

PASTELILLO—20¢

A large half-moon, half-filled turnover with a crisp, fried dough outer covering punctured with air bubbles.

* The frequent orange-yellow color of many Puerto Rican foods is attained b the use of a commercially packaged powdered mixture called Creole Cond ment. It's most prevalent ingredients are cumin, cornflower and annatto see

EASY

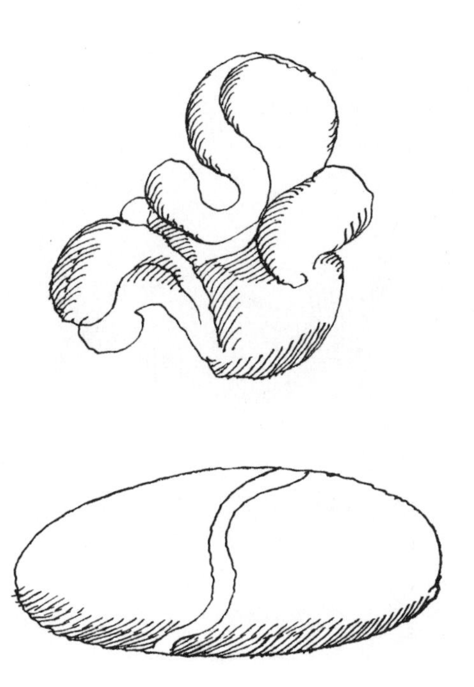

CHICARON—10–25¢

This offering comes, depending on size, in a variety of forbidding baroque shapes. It is simply fried pork rinds. This is the pleasant version of cellophane wrapped smaller sections sold in many delicatessens.

PLANTANO—20¢

A combination of fried nonripe banana and plantain surrounding a filling of ground meat. Sweet and mild in flavor.

INTERMEDIATE

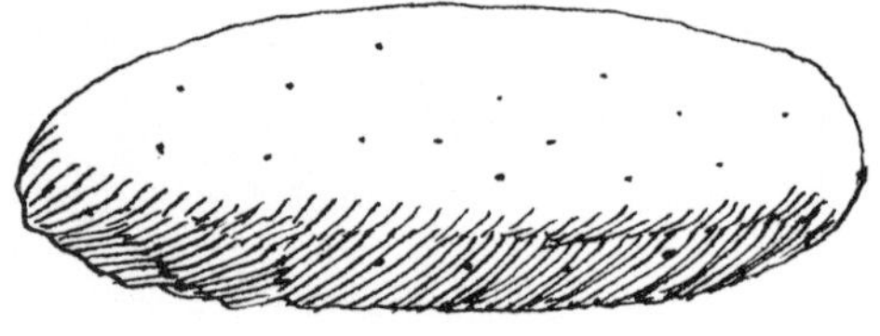

BACALAO—10¢

An orange-colored fried codfish and cornmeal flatcake. Though non-fishy in taste, it tends to be quite salty.

ALCAPURIA—20¢

A dark brown, elliptically shaped mixture of two coarsely ground Latin American tubers, Yucca and Gaulia. It is stuffed with chopped meat and has a pleasant corn-meal-like texture. Flavor is exotic.

INTERMEDIATE

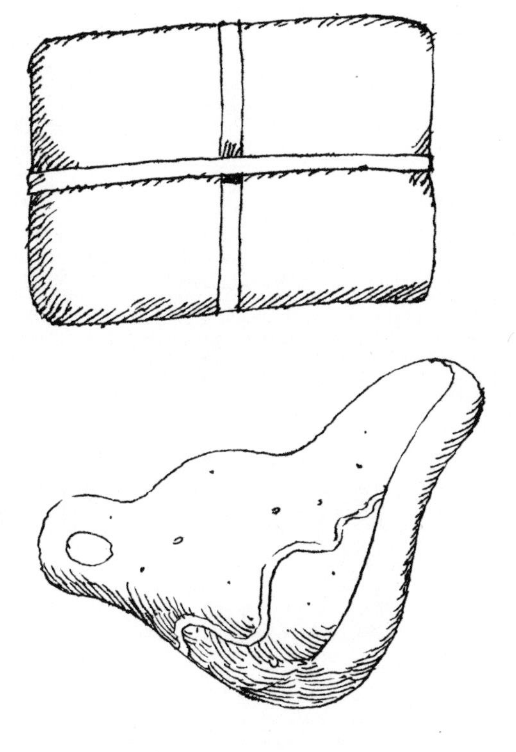

PASTEL—35¢

A neatly tied, parchment-wrapped package containing a combination of three tropical tubers, Yucca, Gaulia and Bahaha. It is boiled, mealy and mild flavored. Best eaten as an accompaniment to more highly spiced foods.

LENGUA—20¢

Pig's tongue, mild and meaty in flavor. It has a rather firm texture similar to the better known beef tongue. Frequently served in a tomato sauce.

DIFFICULT

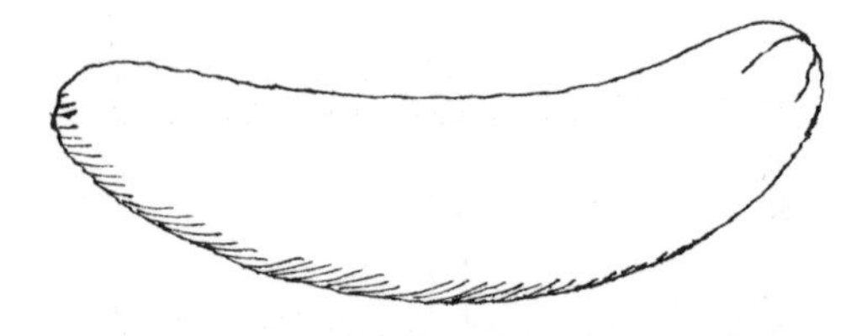

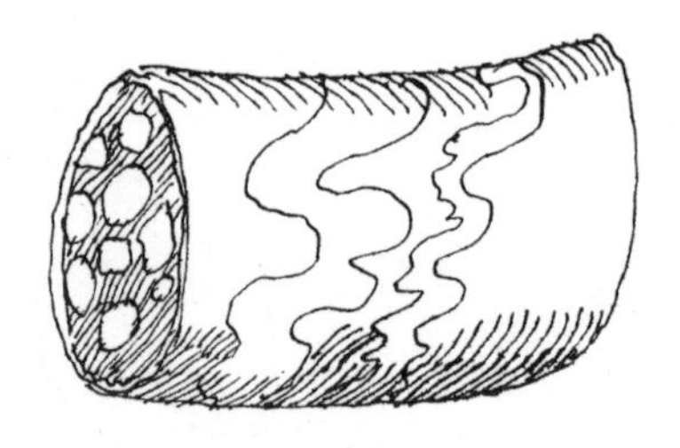

GINEO—10¢

An unripe banana that has been boiled in salted water for about twenty minutes. It is pulpy, potato flavored and very boring.

MORCILLA—15¢

A maroonish red, loosely assembled fat-flecked sausage. It is highly spiced and loaded with Garlic. Separates the Jibaros from the boys.

DIFFICULT

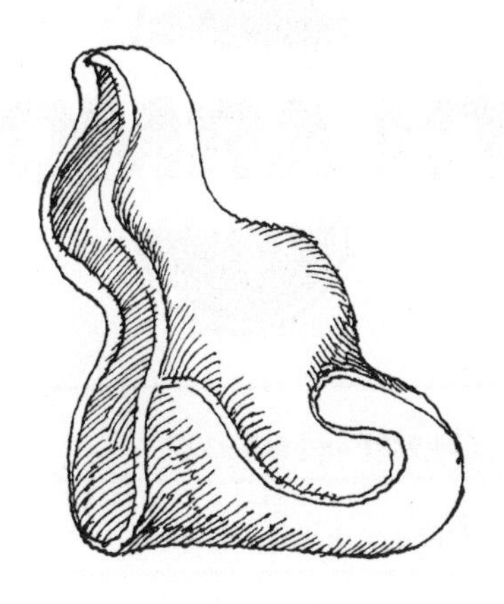

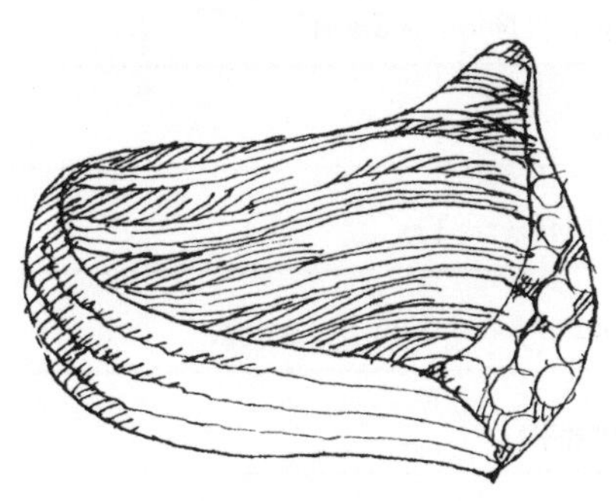

OREJA OR OREJITA—15¢

This mild flavored, grisly object is a pig's ear. It is on the fatty side and cooked in thin tomato sauce.

ESTOMAGO—15¢

As one would guess by the name, this is a sliced pig's stomach. Not unlike tripe but considerably tougher.

Telephone: 684-9301 and 684-9395

Days Open: Monday through Friday

Hours Open: Noon to 3 P.M.

Bar: Yes

Air Conditioning: Yes

Recommended for: Lunch. Dating.

Your Comments:

Food: Poor to Fair

Ambiance: Excellent

Hygiene: Good

Service: Fair to Good

The 69th Regiment Armory Restaurant (26th Street and Lexington Avenue) is included in this book because it is truly underground. Without any indication on the outside, the basement of this formidable fortress houses a roomy, competently managed restaurant. Once you are inside the armory it is best to ask directions. Though the food served in these spacious quarters is fairly ordinary, it is the surrounding mural that makes eating in the armory restaurant unusual and worthwhile. The painting is a visual chronicle of the battle history of the famed 69th Regiment, and deployed on all four walls are hundreds of thrusting, charging, shooting, hiding German and American combatants. One might conclude that dining in the center of this martial turbulence would hardly be a tranquil experience; the curious blandness of the paintings, however, would not give a pacifist a moment's indigestion.

Consistently enough, the cooking at the 69th Regiment restaurant is American style. Characteristic dishes include ham steak with pineapple ring, vegetable, potato and salad for $1.25 (a),* $1.50 (d)†; chopped steak with vegetable, potato and salad for 95 cents (a), $1.25 (d); pork chops with vegetable, potato and salad for $1.45 (a), $1.75 (d); sliced steak with vegetable, potato and salad for $1.65 (a), $1.95 (d); cheese omelet for 95 cents (a), $1.25 (d). The dinner adds soup, dessert and a beverage.

Portions are average. The service is pleasant. The restaurant is open to civilians for lunch only. The evenings are reserved for Guardsmen.

* à la carte
† dinner

Telephone: MU 4-9187

Days Open: 6 days (Closed Sunday)

Hours Open: M. through F., noon to 2 P.M., 5 P.M. to 9 P.M.; Sat., 5 P.M. to 9 P.M.

Bar: Saki, sherry, beer

Air Conditioning: Yes

Recommended for: Lunch. Dating.

Your Comments:

Food: Good to Excellent

Ambiance: Good to Excellent

Hygiene: Good

Service: Fair to Good

Established in 1936, Suehiro, 35 E. 29th Street, is one of the oldest family-run Japanese restaurants in New York. It occupies two parlor floors in a brownstone on an ordinary business side street. The decor of the two rooms is attractively sparse in the characteristic Japanese manner. The outstanding quality of Suehiro is its consistent and orderly sense of proportion. The service is relaxed and efficient. In the evening the waitresses wear the colorful kobe, the native costume of Japan. For those familiar with Japanese food, the menu contains no surprises. Everything on the menu, however, is well prepared, attractively served and tasty. The à la carte list features soybean soup (35 cents); sashimi (delicate slices of raw fish with soy sauce and horseradish) at 85 cents (authors' choice); tanin (beef, egg and vegetables on rice) for $1.00; chail-chali (beef and onions) for $1.00; ten-don (butterfly shrimp on rice) for $1.00; bean curd with ginger sauce for 75 cents. There are complete luncheons such as teishoku, consisting of a choice of soy or clear soup, broiled fish or pork, tempura (butterfly-fried shrimp, vegetable, rice), starting at $1.75. Dinner with an additional dish and a choice of dessert is slightly higher, but one can keep below the $2.00 limit by ordering from the à la carte menu, which remains constant in price.

Japanese portions are adequate but hardly extravagant, and this is not the place to go when extremely hungry. A small bottle of sake (Japanese rice wine) is a good buy at $1.00, although Japanese beer at 70 cents is disproportionately high.

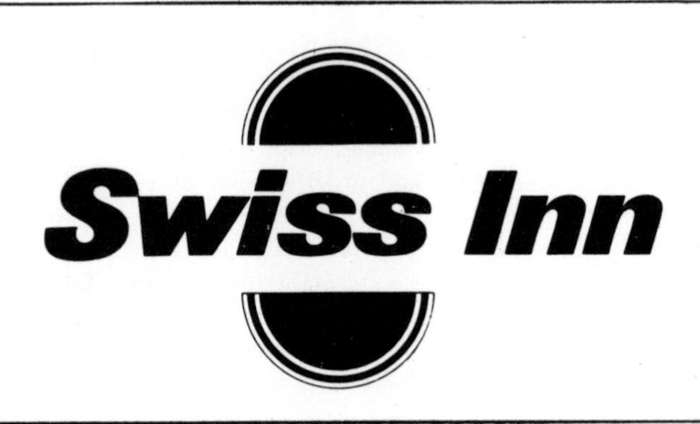

Telephone: CO 5-9283

Days Open: 6 days (Closed Sunday)

Hours Open: M. through F., noon to 2:30 P.M., 5 P.M. to 10 P.M.; Sat., 5 P.M. to 10 P.M.

Bar: Yes

Air Conditioning: Yes

Recommended for: Lunch. Dating.

Your Comments:

Food: Good

Ambiance: Fair to Good

Hygiene: Good

Service: Good to Excellent

The Swiss Inn, 355 W. 46th Street, between Eighth and Ninth Avenues in the theater district, is nestled in a street that literally burgeons with a mixture of restaurants. Most of the establishments on this street are considerably more expensive than this small, authentically Swiss retreat. This modest restaurant consists of two not overly bright rooms. There is a tiny bar in the first room toward the entrance, and the two Swiss sporting dailies hanging from their reading rods lend a nostalgic European note. An equally small room in the rear has about six tables seating some 20 people. In an attempt to overcome any possible claustrophobic feeling the walls are decorated with some rather good *Trompe-l'oeil* murals of Swiss landscapes. To complete the illusion, the painted windows bordering the view are enlivened by the pop addition of real kitchen curtains. The excellent bargains at the Swiss Inn are confined to four items on the luncheon menu. The luncheon consists of a choice of appetizer, entrée, dessert and a beverage. While the choice is limited, the portions are generous and the quality high. Swiss cooking is somewhat eclectic, reflecting French, German and Italian influences. These diverse tendencies are nicely balanced in the dishes offered. Among the appetizers there is an egg à la russe, fruit and vegetable juices and a soup of the day. We had a rich, thick green-pea purée with small chunks of pink ham. It was served properly hot in a small marmite. The four main courses in the *Underground Gourmet* category were distributed between French and German styles—a filet de sole meunière ($1.90), a St. Galler schublig at $2.00 (large red pork sausage), and a reppli with sauerkraut for $2.00 (authors' choice), which is a thick slab of pork loin steamed with sauerkraut and a boiled potato. At $1.90 there is a range of omelets (plain, cheese, ham and mushroom). This dish, while tasty and filling, has a somewhat heavier quality than its French counterpart. All these dishes come with a green vegetable. Accompanying the entrée is the nine-inch circular patty of extremely tasty hashed brown potatoes.

The dessert selection is small but rich. A sweet caramel custard comes topped with a dollop of whipped cream. Meringue glacé, not ordinarily found on a small restaurant menu, is excellent. In this dish a thin crisp meringue surrounds a scoop of vanilla ice cream and is festooned with puffs of good whipped cream. Should these items prove a bit too sweet for some, there is a choice of Emmenthaler or Gruyere cheese. Coffee has a lasting mocha flavor considerably beyond the routine. Swiss Inn service is characteristically Swiss: quick, attentive and courteous.

Telephone:	YU 9-9539
Days Open:	Monday through Friday
Hours Open:	6 A.M. to 5 P.M.
Bar:	No
Air Conditioning:	Yes
Recommended for:	Lunch.
Your Comments:	
Food:	Good
Ambiance:	Poor
Hygiene:	Poor
Service:	Fair to Good

Tannenbaum's, 44 Little West 12th Street, in the shadow of New York's West Side docks, is an unprepossessing luncheonette. It is literally tucked beneath a railroad siding in the very gut of the meat-packing and processing district. Like its Parisian counterpart, Les Halles, this fascinating area (well worth a visit) is a scene of turbulent activity throughout the day as trucks disgorge whole sides of meat which white-smocked, burly butchers unload and send on their way to food lockers. One of the favorite local eating places for the robust crews of meat packers is Tannenbaum's. They go because Tannenbaum's serves generous portions of good-quality, simply prepared meat dishes at prices to fit a workingman's pocket. In all other respects this luncheonette is relatively undistinguished. There is no decor; the counter seats about 15 and the tables accommodate 60 to 70. Some of the good dishes are brisket of beef ($1.45) and very substantial corned beef and cabbage at $1.45 (both authors' choices). Other basic dishes include meat goulash ($1.00), Salisbury steak ($1.25), a fricassee of chicken ($1.25) and finally meatballs and spaghetti (95 cents). The menu also lists a surprising assortment of omelets: green pea, onion, jelly, cream cheese, ham, spinach, mushroom, tongue, western and plain. Normally there are two soups of the day. The home-made lima bean was particularly pleasant for 30 cents (authors' choice). Desserts follow the luncheonette pattern and are commercial in look and taste, but a rather nice apple strudel is available. Coffee, consumed in great quantities, is only ordinary.

Telephone: 243-9946

Days Open: 7 days

Hours Open: 9 A.M. to midnight

Bar: No

Air Conditioning: Yes

Recommended for: Lunch. Dinner. Dating?

Your Comments:

Food: Good

Ambiance: Fair to Good

Hygiene: Fair

Service: Fair to Good

La Taza de Oro (The Gold Cup), 96 Eighth Avenue (between 14t
and 15th streets) is at the beginning of a string of Latin Ameri
can luncheonette–restaurants that runs uptown along Eight
Avenue. Unhappily most of these places are not of high qualit
either in food or general cleanliness. The Taza de Oro is singu
larly superior to its neighborhood contemporaries. While La Taz
falls within the category of a luncheonette, its range of hot, pre
pared entrées is more extensive than one can usually find in thi
type of establishment. The quality of the food is generally goo
and there are several unusual dishes available every day. One o
these is an attractive, pastel-colored octopus salad (author
choice). It is prepared with cold tomato wedges, onions, pepper
and small cylindrical sections of pink and white octopus in oi
and vinegar dressing at $1.25 with rice and beans and 85 cent
for a smaller order of the salad alone. A soup dish that coul
serve very well as an entrée is the delicious tripe soup (70 cents)
Large pieces of chewy tripe are served in a thickened, flavorfu
broth. Admittedly, there is no middle ground between tripe hater
and tripe lovers, but the latter will not be disappointed by thi
dish. There is a full range of Puerto Rican dishes. These includ
pollo asado (roast chicken) for $1.25, camarones (shrimp) fo
$1.50, langosta (lobster) for $1.50, lechone asado (roast pork
for $1.00, carne guisada (beef stew) for $1.25, vieja rop
(shredded beef) for 95 cents (very tasty and an authors' choice)
calamares (clams) for $1.25, liver steak for $1.00. All thes
dishes come with a heaping mound of the inevitable yellow
orange rice and marrow beans. Desserts are routine, but the fla
(25 cents) and the bread pudding (20 cents) are good. Coffee i
strong.

At La Taza great quantities of food are robustly displayed o
a steam table behind the serving counter, and the general tone i
one of a no-nonsense eatery.

In general, La Taza is clean and orderly, but during the lunc
rush (it is also open for dinner) copious amounts of litter ac
cumulate on the floor. The atmosphere is friendly, the service fa
and casual. La Taza de Oro is a workingman's place. In plai
unpretentious surroundings it offers well-cooked, simple, goo
inexpensive food and some pleasant surprises.

Telephone:	734-9881
Days Open:	6 days (Closed Tuesday)
Hours Open:	11 A.M. to 11:30 P.M.
Bar:	No
Air Conditioning:	Yes
Recommended for:	Lunch. Dinner. Dating.
Your Comments:	
Food:	Good to Excellent
Ambiance:	Fair
Hygiene:	Good
Service:	Good

The Tip Top Restaurant, 1489 Second Avenue (at 76th Street), is located on the Hungarian fringe of predominantly German Yorkville. As with so many other good eating finds, the general appearance of this small restaurant is deceptive. The Tip Top looks like any one of the hundreds of conventional luncheonettes that serve the city, perhaps a shade more friendly and cleaner. The first surprise comes upon looking at its menu, which offers an extensive variety of unusual Hungarian dishes. In point of fact there are so many excellent choices on the bill of fare that selection of a few for special commendation is difficult. There is a cold fruit soup (25 cents), a sweet broth of stewed seasonal fresh fruits, that is delicate and beautifully refreshing. The soup is a remarkable buy and an enthusiastic authors' choice. There is a beef goulash soup (60 cents), which is virtually a stew, composed of beef chunks in a creamy brown stock. For many this fine dish, with a slice or two of the accompanying substantial dark bread, makes a perfectly adequate lunch. The Hungarian fish soup (75 cents), made of carp, provides another rare and excellent appetizer. A simple listing of the diverse entrées will indicate the invention and imagination that has gone into the Tip Top menu: Paprika chicken with sour-cream sauce ($1.20), sour lung and heart with bread dumplings and sour cream (95 cents), rumsteak with onions ($1.40). Beef steak with Hungarian lecso is $1.40—lecso is a spicy sausage. Veal goulash with sour cream and spatzle is $1.20—spatzles are chewy, curled egg noodles. Breaded chicken liver is $1.20, roast duckling with steamed cabbage is $1.40. The traditional stuffed cabbage is only $1.20. For the less wealthy there is a good-sized dish of mixed spatzles with egg and salad (60 cents) or a hearty potato goulash with sausage and salad (85 cents).

The portions are liberal, and cooking is light of hand in the best Hungarian tradition. All the dishes come with a serving of potatoes and a deftly vinegared cucumber salad. In many *Underground Gourmet* restaurants the desserts have been something of a disappointment. The Tip Top very happily maintains a consistently high standard in this area as well. The desserts on the menu are superb and truly reflect the Hungarian sweet tooth. There is a dish of two diaphanously thin Hungarian crêpes called palacsinta which come with a choice of walnut, jam or cheese filling for only 40 cents, and a far-out dish, listed as a dessert, is noodles with cheese, sour cream and fried bacon (55 cents).

The menu changes daily, and there are always exciting daily specials to be found. Coffee is the traditional dime, but the espresso is surprisingly high at 25 cents.

The Tip Top is homey, the service is appropriately pleasant and the value is truly exceptional.

Telephone:	889-5385
Days Open:	Monday through Friday
Hours Open:	11 A.M. to 3 P.M.
Bar:	No
Air Conditioning:	Yes
Recommended for:	Lunch. Dating.
Your Comments:	
Food:	Good to Excellent
Ambiance:	Fair to Good
Hygiene:	Fair
Service:	Good

Tonkatsu, 9 E. 32nd Street, is a Japanese restaurant a half flight below street level and open only for lunch. Its menu corresponds to similar establishments, but there are enough differences to make it distinctive. For one thing, the food seems tastier and the portions are larger. If one is hungry an hour after eating Chinese food, hunger sets in ten seconds after a Japanese meal. This is not the case, however, at Tonkatsu.

The menu is divided into two categories—the two-course luncheon and the à la carte section. The luncheon offers a hearty brown bean soup or a beautifully clear broth with slices of floating vegetables, to add taste and interest and to delight the eye. Familiar Japanese dishes on the luncheon include beef, pork or chicken sukiyaki, \$2.50 / \$2.00*; beef, pork or chicken teriyaki, \$2.35 / \$1.80; soy-sauce-marinated broiled slices of any one of the preceding served with vegetables. Tonkatsu, the eponym of the restaurant, is a thin, lightly breaded succulent and satisfying pork cutlet, \$2.35 / \$1.90, an authors' choice. Sashimi, \$2.25 / \$1.60—slices of raw fish—is tasty but not very filling. Yakizakana, fresh fish broiled with salt, is \$2.25 / \$1.60. Tempura, a popular batter-covered deep-fried shrimp with vegetable is \$2.50 / \$2.00. Our favorites are the don-buri dishes, also available on the luncheon. Don-buri means "bowl" in Japanese, and these dishes are various mixtures of meat, eggs and vegetables served over a substantial bed of rice in a great bowl. Katsu-don, sautéed pork cutlet, vegetable and scrambled eggs, is \$1.75. Sukiyaki-don is fundamentally the same but with beef (\$1.75). Oyako-don is the chicken variant (\$1.65). The other types are unagi-don (broiled eel and sauce) at \$1.80; ten-don (fried shrimps and sauce) at \$1.75; Japanese-style curry at \$1.60.

The udon are essentially large bowls of noodles in soup with at least one other ingredient. Niku-udon (sliced pork or beef) is \$1.30, kitsune-udon (fried bean curd) is \$1.00, tsukimi (eggs) are \$1.00, tempura-udon (fried shrimps) are \$1.30, and finally kake-udon, which is nothing more than the noodles all by themselves, are 90 cents. A small side dish of a cold vegetable, generally spinach with sesame sauce, and a light green tea are the

* Two-course luncheon price / à la carte price

accompaniments. The dessert list is minimal, consisting of ic
cream (25 cents), melon (50 cents) and yokan, a very, ver
sweet bean-paste square not unlike guava jelly (35 cents).

Tonkatsu is a large, squarish room, informally decorated wit
plastic bonsai, a Japanese embroidery and an occasional hard
edge abstract painting. A glimpse of the kitchen reveals that th
walls are lined with silver foil. The pleasant service is by wai
resses who are not strong on English. Fortunately one can rel
on pointing at the menu, which has plenty of full-color photo
graphs of most of the dishes.

Telephone: PL 9-6527

Days Open: 7 days

Hours Open: 11:30 P.M. to 8 P.M.

Bar: No

Air Conditioning: Yes

Recommended for: Lunch. Dinner. Dating.

Your Comments:

Food: Good

Ambiance: Fair to Good

Hygiene: Good to Excellent

Service: Excellent

Trefner's, 619 Lexington Avenue (at 53rd Street), is a pale-green and beige tearoom-style restaurant. This well-run establishment has been under the able direction of Mrs. Trefner at this convenient location for over twenty years. The decor bespeaks a bygone period, but the chairs, the wallpaper murals and the mirrored walls look splendidly maintained. For a small restaurant, Trefner's has a surprisingly large staff of three chefs, each with his own special approach. In general, the style of cooking may be termed Hungarian-American. Only table d'hôte luncheons and dinners are offered, and the appetizer and entrée selections run to the familiar and homey. What is particularly impressive is that in this high-rent area one can get a carefully prepared meal of soup, entrée, fresh vegetables, an excellent dessert and a beverage at luncheon or dinner for under $2.00.

At lunch you can begin with a choice of either juice or soup; and the fresh vegetable broth is very good. Two of the most popular dishes are the top sirloin of beef au jus and the Hungarian goulash, both at $1.95. The individual chicken pie with biscuit crust is beautifully prepared with plenty of white meat and comes as part of the complete luncheon for only $1.60 (authors' choice). A good-sized portion of old-fashioned lamb stew with fresh vegetables is $1.80 (authors' choice). Other good dishes are the roast loin of Jersey pork with apple sauce ($1.95), chicken liver and mushroom omelet ($1.75), chicken paprika Hungarian style ($1.75), pepper steak with steamed rice ($1.80) and roast-beef hash with fried egg ($1.65). Dinner is more expensive, but between the price range of $1.85 to $2.50 there are eleven excellent choices, including roast chicken with cranberry sauce, Southern-style fried chicken, broiled calf's liver with onions, creamed sweetbreads in patty shell, boiled beef tongue with fresh spinach, and chicken croquettes with gravy.

As mentioned before, desserts are truly excellent. All baking is done on the premises under the supervision of a baker who has a really light hand with the pies, cakes and biscuits. We can recommend the green apple pie with whipped cream (real), butterscotch cream pie, maple nut layer cake à la mode, blueberry tart, coconut cream pie (authors' choice) and old-fashioned peach shortcake with whipped cream. Coffee is good.

The service is unusually swift, with a pleasant concern for niceties. You won't meet any hipsters at Trefner's, but you will get good value, good food and good service.

Telephone:	LE 2-5567
Days Open:	6 days (Closed Sunday)
Hours Open:	8 A.M. to 7 P.M.
Bar:	No
Air Conditioning:	Yes
Recommended for:	Lunch.
Your Comments:	
Food:	Excellent
Ambiance:	Good
Hygiene:	Fair to Good
Service:	Good

Trinacria (Importing Co.), 415 Third Avenue (at 29th Street), is a fascinating store that sells imported cheeses, olive oil, sardines, candied fruit, tortellini, amaretti, pine cones, spices, pulverized Turkish coffee, poppadums, curry, Polish hams, smoked oysters, espresso machines, cast-iron Dutch ovens, omelet pans, cheese and coffee grinders, machinetti, soda, imported beer and thousands of other familiar and unfamiliar items. The vast assortment of products is a pleasantly organized chaos. The cheeses, salamis and kitchenware hang from above, and the walls and aisles are stocked from floor to ceiling. The smells are a stimulating mixture of Parmesan cheese, dried sausage, fragrant spices and, above all, the aroma of cooking veal, sausage, eggplant, tomatoes and peppers. The last named are some of the ingredients used in the making of what the cognoscenti believe to be the best hero sandwiches in New York. This belief, with which the authors concur, is supported most convincingly in their range of hot sandwiches which are freshly prepared every day. These include veal and peppers, meatball, sausage and peppers, egg and peppers, potato and eggs, and eggplant.

Handsome Mrs. Romano presides with a regal cool over the row of red cast-iron casseroles which line the counter. With a watchful concern she sees that the bubbling sauces are filled to the proper level and maintained at just the right temperature. Mr. Bono, a slight, somewhat remote man, supervises, slices and prepares sandwiches made of the excellent variety of cold meats and cheeses. These items include many popular domestic products and an array of imported mortadella, salami, prosciutto, provolone, taleggio, cappicolla and mozzarella. In both the hot and cold sandwiches the management encourages fanciful combinations. We recommend veal and eggplant, egg and peppers with thin slices of prosciutto or simply the classic mixed meat and cheese that includes a slice of everything (cold) as well as a sprinkling of Trinacria's home-made pickled Italian salad (available separately at 20 cents for ¼ lb.)—watch out for the unpitted olives! The sandwiches are served on either nine-inch-long Italian bread or a smaller Italian sesame-seeded roll. The hot sandwiches may include a liberal showering of grated Parmesan cheese. The prices for the larger version either hot or cold ranges from 60 to 90 cents. The smaller kind is proportionately less and can go as low as 30 cents.

The big problem at Trinacria is where to eat the sandwich once you have it. The best bet is to take the sandwich with you to either a convenient nearby bench or to your office or home. Trinacria offers the alternative of walking to the rear of the store and eating your sandwich while standing in the cramped aisle. The management also permits you to rest your sandwich on any vacant counter space if you can find it. Admittedly, this is an uncivilized way of eating a sandwich of such high quality, but Trinacria's customers seem to bear it without complaint.

Coffee is available, as well as almost any imaginable soda or beer, obtained from the self-service refrigerator case. On a warm spring day a Trinacria sandwich, a bottle of beer and a park bench (Madison Square Park is nearby—26th Street and Madison Avenue) is an unbeatable New York combination.

SEE ERRATA, page 5

Telephone: TR 4-8950
Days Open: 6 days (Closed Monday)
Hours Open: 11:30 A.M. to 10:30 P.M.
Bar: Beer and wine
Air Conditioning: Yes
Recommended for: Lunch. Dinner. Dating.
Your Comments:
Food: Excellent
Ambiance: Good
Hygiene: Excellent
Service: Good

Trini, 271 Amsterdam Avenue (at 73rd Street), is a tidy, first-rate restaurant whose location near Lincoln Center makes it especially attractive as a pre-concert spot for dining. In addition to its geographical convenience Trini offers a package of other virtues. Frequently, restaurants that meet *Underground Gourmet* standards on the basis of quality and reasonable prices suffer from defects in other areas. This unusual Latin-American restaurant, however, is virtually unflawed. It is spanking clean, the service is cordial, the menu is inventive, the food is beautifully prepared and the prices are very low. If there were more places like this model restaurant, life in New York would be considerably enhanced. The excellence of Trini's is due to the dedication and pride of its proprietor, Mr. Vincent Lopez, a warm and friendly man who for fourteen years has demonstrated his knowledge of Latin-American cuisine at this spot.

A vanishing phenomenon, the tax-free 99-cent lunch, is still available at Trini. The full-course luncheon menu includes a choice of soup (the lima bean is sensational), juice or fruit cup. One can then choose from an excellent list of entrées which includes onion omelet, chilerama (a fried egg covered with chili con carne on a bed of rice), baked breast of lamb, stuffed meat loaf with rice and salad, fresh beef tongue with rice and beans, and picadillo (described on page 48). If you wish to escalate your check to $1.20, Trini offers an additional choice of tuna-fish salad; tamales; rice and beans; pot roast, rice and salad; and beef stew. The desserts are various fruit pies, excellent homemade cakes, and coco-loco (Mr. Lopez's inspired combination of shredded coconut and bread pudding, blended into a smooth mixture without any loss of the grainy bread texture)—an authors' choice. Pineapple milk pudding is a delightful ice cream-like confection—an authors' choice.

The dinner menu offers a variety of unconventional and interesting dishes. Mr. Lopez's pride is the Venezuelan hallaca, a mixture of chicken, pork, vegetables and spices enveloped in a covering of steamed corn meal. The corn used is of a special imported variety, ground by hand on Mexican grinding stones that Mr. Lopez brought with him from Mexico some fourteen years ago. The dish takes several days to prepare and the result is impressive. Hallaca is served with black beans and white rice at $1.95 (authors' choice). A tender lamb shank Spanish-style, prepared with onions, green peppers and tomatoes, is served with yellow rice and red beans at $1.75 (authors' choice). Other fascinating dishes are shredded beef, rice, beans and fried bananas ($1.90); Dominican sausages with plantain ($1.85); Cuban tamal, rice and beans ($1.70); pork chop à la Creole ($1.95); liver à la Trini and Spanish sausage ($1.90); rice and squid or sardines ($1.65); Spanish sausage omelet ($1.25); potato and onion omelet ($1.00). A special section of Mexican dishes includes, among others, puebla chicken mole (a spicy sauce with a chocolate base) at $2.30; three tamales or tacos ($1.90); a Mexican combo—one taco, one tamale, rice and beans ($1.90). The dinner desserts are the same as those served on the luncheon. For 75 cents more than the cost of an entrée Mr. Lopez has the standing offer to throw in soup, fresh salad, dessert, coffee and a glass of wine (white or red)! An irresistible bargain. The Trini staff has been with the restaurant almost since its inception; consequently there is a pleasant, professional ease about the service. Latin-American restaurants generally have good coffee, and Trini carries the tradition forward nobly.

Telephone:	CA 6-8133
Days Open:	7 days
Hours Open:	Noon to 3 A.M.
Bar:	Beer and wine
Air Conditioning:	Yes
Recommended for:	Lunch. Dinner. Dating.
Your Comments:	
Food:	Good
Ambiance:	Fair
Hygiene:	Fair to Good
Service:	Poor

Vincent's Clam Bar, 119 Mott Street, is a seafood restaurant and bar located in the predominantly Italian section of Manhattan bounded by Greenwich Village on the north and Chinatown on the south. The restaurant is a bubbling, steamy room flanked by a bar on one side and a dining counter and open kitchen lining the opposite wall. There is another room with tables in the rear, but the counter is the interesting place to eat. Vincent's concise menu of five dishes is prepared to order before you in vats of boiling oil and pots of steaming broth. The basic five items all offered at 95 cents a serving are fried shrimps, fried squid, steamed mussels, steamed scungilli and raw clams. The dishes are simply served with bread or biscuit and a choice of two degrees of hot tomato sauce: very hot and too hot. All dishes are tasty, but the authors preferred the scungilli and squid. Scungilli (a dialectal version of concighlie) is a southern Italian delicacy. It is the meat of the whelk, gray in color, delicate in flavor and somewhere between abalone and octopus in taste. This dish is generally confined to the menus of Neapolitan and Sicilian restaurants.

Portions are modest, though three servings shared by two people appeared to be adequate. Vincent's serves only one brand of an ordinary domestic beer; however, it is more than welcome as a quenching agent because of the fiery nature of the sauce.

Vincent's is always crowded and the turnover is brisk, and you should not expect sensitive attention. Despite this allowance, the counter service seemed unnecessarily curt and even bordered on the rude. There are no desserts or coffee on the menu, but a short walk up Mott Street will bring you to Ferrara's, where a splendid range of Italian pastries, ice cream and coffees is served.

Telephone:	GR 7-2858
Days Open:	7 days
Hours Open:	M. through Th., 8 A.M. to 7 P.M.; F. 8 A.M. to 5 P.M.; Sat., Sun., 8 A.M. to 8 P.M.
Bar:	No
Air Conditioning:	Yes
Recommended for:	Lunch. Dinner.
Your Comments:	
Food:	Good
Ambiance:	Good
Hygiene:	Poor to Fair
Service:	Good

Yonah Schimmel's Knishes Bakery, 137 E. Houston Street, is a remnant of another era. This quiet little bakery–restaurant evokes the time when tens of thousands of Jewish immigrants found a friendly haven on the lower East Side. Now, a half century later, this area has changed its character. Puerto Ricans, the newest wave of immigrants, have brought their Latin-American culture to this traditionally Jewish neighborhood, and the vestigial Jewish shopkeepers have had to adapt by adding Spanish to their linguistic repertoire, while the Puerto Rican has added the knish to his gustatory pleasures.

The origial Yonah was the "shamus" (sexton) of the local Roumanian synagogue when he established this bakery in 1910. Since his death, the business has been operated by his grandchildren. Their debt to the patriarchial Yonah is symbolized by their display of his portrait in the bakery's window. The *raison d'être* of this landmark has always been and is today the potato knish. Although the knish has played an active role in many New York political campaigns,* some readers may still never have seen or eaten one.

The authentic hand-made knish made at Yonah Schimmel's is an irregularly shaped, fat, bunlike amalgam of mashed potatoes, flour and onions, all encased in a thin, crisp, brown pastry skin, and as a food contains great stomach-filling properties. As is the custom with simple dishes, the knish is at its best when fresh, hot and made of ingredients of good quality. The mass-produced commercial knish most often encountered in New York delicatessens lacks these essentials. It can be recognized immediately by a thick, embossed surfaced of an unnaturally yellow hue. Another clue to its identification is its hard-edged rectangular shape. Because the commercial knish is often kept on a hot grill for days at a time, the potato filling tends to go sour. The real tragedy of this abuse is that many people brought up on this inferior product have never known a real knish. Yonah Schimmel's is perhaps the last bastion of the genuine item. Yet, this brave restaurant lives mainly on its past glory. Izzy Finklestein, the waiter who has

* No New York politician in the last 50 years has been elected to public office without having at least one photograph showing him on the lower East Side with a knish in his face.

been with Yonah's for 45 years, recalls the day when Mrs. Roosevelt came in to order a bag of knishes for her husband, Franklin, who was campaigning in the district. "On Sundays, rich people, very rich people, used to come in their cars and they would wait on line for hours to get in." A more recent regular visitor was former Mayor Robert F. Wagner. Now the restaurant is run down, almost seedy and full of nostalgia.

The dining room is small and plain and the 50-year-old wood-framed glass showcase at the entrance has been painted over at least at hundred times. Arranged along the side walls like hurdles are the long, narrow formica-topped tables. Silverware, like a metallic bouquet, is kept in glass containers on the tables. Other room decorations are small mirrors, and two ancient electric fans. Knishes are ordered from the store-long kitchen beneath the dining room. They are sent up promptly and piping hot by means of a dumbwaiter.

Purists consider knishes other than potato an affront, but in the interest of non-partisan reportage the other types should be listed. One is kasha (a heavy lump of cooked buckwheat groats), which—if it can be imagined—is even more filling than the potato type. The cheese, blueberry cheese and cherry cheese are really knish mutants. They are closer in taste and appearance to what we know as Danish pastry. The cheese varieties are really more suitable as desserts. Apart from the sandwiches, which are undistinguished, the remaining offering is the "potatonik," which was called "spudnik" during the early days of Russian space accomplishments. Potatonik is essentially a baked-potato pudding. A large oleaginous square costs 20 cents. All knishes are 25 cents each, potato being the obvious authors' choice. Mr. Finklestein, our waiter–historian, remembers with a sigh when knishes cost three cents. To wash it all down, soft drinks are available, and a decent cup of coffee is served for only 10 cents. Service is simple and quick.

Beyond the pleasant remembrance of things past, a visit to Yonah Schimmel's bakery is rewarded by those things the *Underground Gourmet* values most highly: good quality at low prices.

Telephone:	734-9555
Days Open:	6 days (Closed Tuesday)
Hours Open:	M., W. through Sat., noon to 9 P.M.; Sun., 11 A.M. to 9 P.M.
Bar:	Beer and wine
Air Conditioning:	No
Recommended for:	Lunch. Dinner. Dating.
Your Comments:	
Food:	Fair to Good
Ambiance:	Good
Hygiene:	Good
Service:	Good

The Yorkville Hungarian Restaurant, 350 E. 81st Street, is in reality a cafeteria, one of the very few ethnic self-service eating places in the city. It is a long, sprawling room with flamboyant modernistic lighting fixtures and a handsome old tiled floor. The plastic flowers provide a rather touching decorative note. The serving counter is at the far end of the room where the proprietors, Mr. and Mrs. Unger and son, solicitously attend to the customers' orders. The menu consists of a small group of basic Hungarian dishes prepared in simple homelike style. Though the choices are small, the items are attractive, and within the limited range everyone should be able to find something to his liking. There are always two or three soups (30 cents each)—one typical example is string-bean soup made of a vegetable base and liberally filled with fine fresh string beans. Chicken soup and fruit soups are also generally available. The kolbas (Hungarian sausage) and peppers is a sturdy peasant dish for $1.55, as is the meat loaf for $1.50. The inevitable gulyash is $1.50. The roasts include a half chicken (with a light, tasty stuffing) duck and pork, all at $1.60. These dishes, as with all others, are served with a choice of two well-cooked vegetables and a choice of a mixed or cucumber salad, the latter being a rather peppery concoction. Sauerbraten is $1.55. Veal cutlet, lamb chops, schnitzel, liver and boiled beef represent a fair sample of the meat entrées and are priced from $1.45 to $1.65. The Ungers are particularly proud of their spareribs and sauerkraut ($1.60). Four omeletes—mushroom, Spanish, Western and cheese—from 90 cents to $1.00 fill out the lower end of the price scale. For dessert there is pastry which looks somewhat like the familiar Danish varieties, rice pudding, melon in season and a truly noteworthy popular neighborhood favorite, palacsinta (pa-la-chinta), at 25 cents, a Hungarian crêpe with cheese or jam filling. The palacsinta, if not on display in the steam table, will be made to your order. An order of three or four can make an excellent meal in itself.

The Yorkville Hungarian Restaurant food is serviceable and portions are substantial. Like other cafeterias it suffers from the problem of keeping food hot throughout the day without losing its flavor. It doesn't always succeed. A rare feature of this cafeteria is the availability of wine, and one *mittel*-European delight is the spritzer (wine and siphon soda) for only 25 cents or 40 cents, depending on size. This indigenous restaurant is roomy, friendly and comfortable. The food is a cut above the usual cafeteria fare, and some of it can be very good indeed.

Short Takes

BALKAN ARMENIAN, 129 E. 27th Street MU 4-8872, MU 9-7925. One of New York's best Armenian restaurants. Stuffed eggplant is superb. Recommended for lunch only. Generally crowded.

BELMORE CAFETERIA, 407 Park Avenue South LE 2-0511. Big, noisy, flashy taxi drivers' hangout. Good jumbo sandwiches. French toast early on Sunday morning is excellent.

BRAZILIAN CLUB RESTAURANT, 150 W. 49th Street 246-4877. Dark, comfortable room. Excellent daily luncheon specials. Authentic and tasty Brazilian cuisine. Good Portuguese wine list.

CHEZ NAPOLEON, 365 W. 50th Street CO 5-6980. An attractive, intimate bistro. Prices are slightly above *Underground Gourmet* limits but represent excellent value for a New York French restaurant. Cooking has a light touch. Great sole. Recommended for luncheon. Bar.

CHOCK FULL O' NUTS. Counter restaurants widely dispersed throughout city. Cream cheese and nut on raisin bread is unsurpassed. Soup and frankfurters also excellent. No tipping.

DIXIE KITCHEN, 1 E. 48th Street EL 5-6265. Forty-one-year-old, slightly seedy underground cafeteria. Fried chicken, pork chops and corn bread, all excellent. Prices low.

EL CORTIJO, 18 W. Houston Street 473-9095. Pleasant, relaxed Spanish bar–restaurant. Luncheon paella specialty is a best buy.

EL FARO, 823 Greenwich Street CH 2-9566. Popular, dark, smoky West Village hangout. Unusual Spanish dishes. Recommended for lunch. Bar.

EL MUNDIAL, 222 W. 116th Street 864-9213. Well-established, neat Spanish restaurant. Surroundings are comfortable, fare is dependable. Beer and wine.

GEFEN'S DAIRY RESTAURANT, 297 Seventh Avenue WA 4-1977. Clean, lively luncheonette–restaurant. Good sour-cream dishes.

JOE'S, 1017 Third Avenue 838-9693. Modified Italian menu. Big portions. Best for lunch. Bar.

JULIO'S, 129 E. 15th Street AL 4-1838. Tiny, crowded below-street-level room. Prices incredibly low. Food tolerable. Popular with students. Wine and beer.

KASHMIR, 108 W. 45 Street 247-8785, CI 6-2289. Indian-Pakistani food. The businessman's luncheon at $1.25 is a great buy. Prices go up considerably for dinner. Beer and wine.

LUIGINO PIZZERIA, 147 W. 48th Street 586-9617. Oldest pizzeria in Broadway area. A wide selection of pizza and pasta. Long room with plenty of booths. Always crowded.

LUNA'S, 112 Mulberry Street CA 6-8657. Southern Italian cooking, which means lots of oil, garlic and tomatoes. Portions are generous; especially good for fried calamari. Beer and wine.

MEXICAN GARDENS, 137 Waverly Place CH 2-9814. Unpretentious, downstairs room. Good, low-priced Mexican specialties. Combination platter offers a nice variety. Imported Mexican beer.

MITCHEL'S MUNICH INN, 332 Bleecker Street 989-3072. Small, clean, pleasant German-style restaurant. Limited menu. Best on unusual cold platters and salads. Imported beer and wine.

OLD GARDEN, 15 W. 29th Street LE 2-8323. Large, crowded, American-style restaurant. Meets *Underground Gourmet* price standards for luncheon only. Large entrée selection and good old-fashioned desserts.

PILGRIM, 49 E. 10th Street 475-9260, 677-9929. Candlelit room. Prices marginal; food American-style–Continental. Interesting waiters and clientele. Uneven.

PINK TEA CUP, 310 Bleecker Street. Soul-food luncheonette by a motherly staff. Sloppy but friendly surroundings. Popular with West Village crowd.

RAPOPORT'S DAIRY RESTAURANT, 93 Second Avenue 477-9338. East Side fixture for many decades. Food undistinguished but filling. Plenty of good rolls, butter and chick-peas. Try the cabbage soup. No bar.

SALON GALIANO, 198 Columbus Avenue TR 4-9704. Cuban luncheonette–restaurant. Standard Latin fare, but try the Cuban sandwiches. First-rate flan and espresso.

SHANGHAI CAFE, 3217 Broadway MO 2-1990. Under the el. Popular with North Chinese food fanciers. Uneven but worth the trip.

SHUN LEE, 119 E. 23rd Street GR 3-4447. Ask for large à la carte menu, which features many unusual specialties. Some dishes are slightly high but good choice falls within *Underground Gourmet* range. Complete dinner and luncheon menu only ordinary.

THE SOUP BAR, 38th Street and Fifth Avenue WI 7-3300. On the tenth floor of Lord & Taylor. Serves soup and apple pie only. Both filling and first-rate.

TAD'S Well-known chain of one-dish, one-price self-service restaurants. Steak, salad, potato for $1.29. Steaks are tough but value is hard to beat.

TEL-AVIV, 171 E. Broadway OR 7-4420. Scrupulously kosher (glatt) full-scale restaurant. Features ample 99-cent luncheon. Dinner prices scale upward but are still quite low.

THOMFORDE'S, 351 W. 125th Street UN 5-0015, 864-9465. Harlem's oldest ice-cream parlor. Customary luncheon fare. Home-made ice cream is sensational. Decor authentically old-fashioned.

TIEN TSIN, 569 W. 125th Street MO 6-5710, 663-9995. Northern Chinese fare. Plain room, excellent food. Popular with students.

TRI-BORO, 1807 Second Avenue 722-9737. German-Irish bar–restaurant. Soccer-player hangout. Corned beef and cabbage a specialty. Beer and ale.

WAH KEE, 16 Doyers Street BE 3-8582. Subterranean, smoky Cantonese-style Chinese eatery. Big portions, good variety, popular.

ZUM ZUM, Pan Am Building Main Concourse 974-6786. Handsomely designed, slick Restaurant Associates neo-German sausage emporium. Stand-up and counter service only. Hot wurst sandwiches, good cold platters. No dinner. Always jammed.

INDEX BY LOCATION

EAST SIDE BELOW 14TH STREET

EAST SIDE 14TH-34TH STREET

EAST SIDE 42ND-59TH STREET

EAST SIDE 59TH-86TH STREET

INDEX BY NATIONALITY